NO FILTER...STORIES BETTER LEFT UNTOLD
By Jeff Worley

INTRODUCTION

Friends,

Warning, you have entered into dangerous territory. To survive this journey you must have been here in the beginning and you must have a sense of humor and thick skin. If not, God bless you and read no further. This book is a true work of comedy and tragedy and where tragedy is comedic. This is my personal collection of bizarre but true stories spanning over 20 years on the road with my band, *Jackyl*. I have seen some real characters come and go through the years and the theme stays the same: funny shit! To set the record straight, this is not your run of the mill "rock star tells all" composition. There will be no mud-slinging, just classic sex, drugs, and rock and roll.

Growing up, not only did I watch my favorite rock stars and musicians, but I had an appetite for comedy. From Richard Pryor to Monty Python to the boozy shenanigans of the live rat pack performances, my sense of humor and my life were influenced. I have spent my life trying to be a decent musician and an adequate guitar player. Don't get me wrong, I've done pretty damn good, but I've always been told, "*You should be a comedian*". I'm not so sure about that. And as the saying goes, "*One man's trash is another man's treasure*", which is why I needed to put these stories on paper. So here's the deal. Some of you may find these stories funny and some of you may find them disturbing, and that's okay. My truths will set you free, mula-fuckas!

With that being said, these are true events that have happened in my life, so y'all don't shoot the messenger. And if your funny bone gets tickled, you can thank me later. Of course, some names have been changed to protect the innocent, and the not so innocent, with me being the most innocent one involved. So sit back and savor my unfiltered past.

Happy reading,

CHAPTER ONE

YOU BOYS AREN'T FROM AROUND HERE, ARE YOU?

Amsterdam

When someone says, *"You ain't from around here, are you?"* they're saying one thing; you're different. Being from the south and having a southern accent, I can understand why people would think that. I take it as a compliment because I *am* different. (You be the judge.) That same question not only starts the book, but it started my career.

Before our first real European tour, Geffen Records sent us to Amsterdam for three days. They set up interviews, meetings with European record executives and booked a show for us. At the time, we were very aware of the legal and high quality of marijuana and hash that Amsterdam had to offer. But we had two rules during that trip: Don't bring shit* in and don't bring shit out. In America, the TSA agents are basically rent-a-cops with a can of mace. The security guys in Europe have fucking machine guns and enormous German Shepherd dogs. But thankfully, we made it through security and arrived in Amsterdam with no problems. The minute our feet hit the ground, we were off to a coffee shop called The Bull Dog Cafe'. My dumb ass went straight to the counter and said, *"Give me the strongest shit you have."* They kindly obliged. The six of us each bought an ounce for our three-day stay in Amsterdam. As the band enjoys diversity, we each bought different strains of weed. We sat down in the cafe' and began to get as high as possible. Not only did we roll joints from each strain, but we also started to blend our own. I liked to call it a *tossed salad*. When the smoke cleared, the munchies set in. One genius in the group blurted out, *"I saw a Burger King on the way here. I've always wanted to smoke a joint in Burger King."* We knew it wasn't "illegal" but we soon found out smoking weed in Burger King was strongly frowned upon. Someone who spoke English approached us and let us know that it wasn't cool to smoke in there but that we could smoke as much as we wanted in our hotel room. So of course, we headed back to our hotel and smoked our asses off. Unknowingly, the strain I ordered was the stuff that made you sleep. Sleep? Hell, that strain could have knocked out an elephant! I slept for more than six hours, woke up and continued to get high again.

That night, we walked around the infamous Red Light District. If you had money, you could get anything from heroin to a prostitute. Most of us were perfectly happy with our weed but there were a select few who decided to travel down those alternative paths.* We left those few and explored the different pubs in town where we got a real education on European beer. We had a blast getting drunk on some great beer that night.

The next day, we got a lesson on European bums. While standing near a bus stop, a weird, dirty Dutch guy came up to us, kind of side stepping up to the street and rips his pants down to his ankles. He started to piss in the streets. We thought it was funny as hell but the locals paid him no attention. When he finished, he just stood there with his "thang" hanging out. Two cops arrived and jerked the guy's pants up so hard that he came two feet off the ground. They threw him in a patrol car and off they went. We knew then it was going to be a hell of a weekend.

*Going all the way – A split second conscious decision to abandon all practical thinking and dive head first into a pool of debauchery and immoral actions that are fueled by copious amounts of drugs and alcohol.

Later that night, the record company was going to take us to a real Chinese restaurant. Not one of those "Americanized" places. This place was Chinese to the core. Traditionally in a Chinese restaurant, you don't order what you want, you're at the mercy of the chef. My brother, Chris, who can't stand to experiment with food, winced when they brought out an appetizer of goose eggs with curry and saffron. You should have seen his face. They brought the golden colored eggs out on a tray that was the size of a car hood. There must have been 50 eggs on that tray. They weren't bad, but they weren't exactly good either. For the main course, they served fried goose, which had laid those golden eggs. (I shit you not!) A lot of the crewmembers were good ole' southern boys who were raised only on their mama's southern cooking. Needless to say, we made a trip back to Burger King just so they could eat (this time without the weed). Afterward, we went straight to our show. It was our last night in Amsterdam.

The next morning, we were scheduled to leave the hotel at 9:00 AM. Before we left, we met in my hotel room to smoke up as much weed as we could before leaving Amsterdam. It was more than we could handle. We had to leave a $5,000 (in U.S. dollars) "pyramid" of weed on the hotel room table. Reminding everyone of the rules, NO WEED ON THE PLANE, we got through the machine gun security and barking dogs and all the scary shit of leaving a foreign country and boarded the plane. One of the crewmembers leaned over and said, *"Dude, I brought some weed and seeds."* I freakin' flipped out. We might have made it through European security but we still had to make it through U.S. Customs. That idiot had rolled the weed in duct tape, stuck it in his ass and duct taped his ass together. Halfway through the flight, he had to shit and asked for my help. I said, *"Man, I can't help you."* After an uncomfortable amount of time in the bathroom, he returned to his seat with a grunt. I made a trip to the bathroom afterwards and found a pile of duct tape with a carpet of pubic hair on the floor. What an idiot! When we landed, you could see him sweating bullets as we approached security. I knew he was going to get busted. But no shit, he made it through customs without a hitch.

After landing at La Guardia, we had a five hour layover. We said, fuck it, let's get high. So out the front gate we went where we found a scheduled bus stop. We found a soda can that we made a pipe out of. Some of the crew were mad because we didn't include them. But you can't have 20 guys in a bus stop passing the fucking peace pipe now can you? It was a covert operation at its best. Later that night, we boarded a 767 that was completely empty. They must have been moving the plane from New York to Atlanta because we were the only passengers on board. The pilots were really young and told us they had just gotten out of the military. I felt pretty confident. They asked us how fast we wanted to get to Atlanta. I asked them what they meant. They said, *"Well, if you don't mind a few bumps, we can get you there pretty quickly."* I said, *"Punch it!"* I swear that was the fastest I have ever flown in a plane. That plane was shaking and bumping around. No doubt there were speed records broken on that flight. I realized how easy the pilots take it on passengers but how much the plane could really take. It was the perfect ending to my first European adventure.

*Shit - Any drug or contraband that may or may not be carried in or on a person across international borders.

<> <> <>

The American Dream ... In Germany?

In 1994, we arrived in Frankfurt, Germany as part of *Jackyl's* European tour to open for Aerosmith. Once we checked into our hotel, we were all suffering from jet lag and unable to sleep. A few of us were "jonesing" for a joint and didn't want to miss one fucking minute of Germany. None of us spoke a word of German so we had our hotel clerk call a taxi. The taxi arrived ... it was a Mercedes-Benz. Beautiful! We managed to tell the driver that we were in the market for a little weed with the universal toking gesture. The driver took us directly to the Red Light District and dropped us off at what turned out to be a methadone clinic. There were guys with needles in their arms who were strung out and lying on the street. Just steps away were some guys throwing dice against a building. They were exchanging money and yelling at each other. Seconds later, several cop cars arrived and we were certain they were there to bust the drug addicts. But they walked right past the addicts and made their way to the gamblers. It was then I knew I wasn't in South Carolina anymore.

Not knowing where to begin our Red Light District adventure, we decided on an international icon ... a strip club. It was nothing like American strip clubs where most of the girls are beautiful and it was much more expensive. After one beer, we decided to leave. The only problem was you couldn't leave through the same door you came in so we had to use a back exit that led to a room filled with vending machines. They weren't your every day vending machines, they were "toy" machines ... sex toys. They were filled with movies, oils, jellies and jams, vibrators, butt plugs ... you name it. Never seeing anything like this, we were all laughing and getting a big kick out of it. When I turned around, there was an enormous billboard with two Vietnamese boys having sex. (I shit you not.) Shocked, and also noticing security cameras, we turned and left. Once out on the street we saw two very large German security men in suits that opened the exit door and were staring at us. We started to walk faster. Out of nowhere, sort of like a voice of God, in a more country accent than mine, someone shouted at us. *"Hey! You boys aren't from around here are you?"* Turning around, I saw a short black man standing in between the two huge German security guards. I said, *"Excuse me?"* He said, *"With those accents, where in the hell are you from?"* I said, *"I'm from Seneca, South Carolina. We're all southern boys here."* He extended his hand and said, *"Me too. I'm from Charlotte, North Carolina."* It turns out this guy had been in the Army for 30 years and married a German girl. After retiring from the Army, he took over his father-in-law's strip club business. He owned clubs all over Germany. The best description of this guy was that he looked and acted like the comedian Kat Williams.

He said to us, *"What the hell are you country boys doing here?"* After explaining our needs to him, he told us that regular pot was hard to find around there. He said, *"Come back later tonight and I'll see what I can do."* We went back to the hotel and got some rest. After a quick rally, we headed back to the strip club. The club owner was extremely generous and cooler than shit! We partied like a son of a bitch all night and we didn't have to pay a cent. At the end of the night, he gave us some parting gifts. He handed me a block of Black Turkish Hash the size of a cell phone. The high off of this hash was different. You would be just as high if you were smoking death weed but you were very energized. The only warning that came with these gifts was: *"Don't get caught at the border."* You will learn more about that warning in a later story. If you're reading this book, Brother, thanks for the hook-up and the story.

<> <> <>

God Saved the Queen But He Couldn't Save the Tour Manager

After leaving Germany, we were off to England. We were set up for more shows with Aerosmith and some with ZZ Top. After a few days, our label appointed tour manager got the full *Jackyl* exposure. Let me explain. First, this guy was dressed in full black leather. He wore this outfit for four straight days, up until the point when he quit. Second, not that there is anything wrong with it, but he was *very* gay. We had worn our English tour manager out. I don't think it was as much of our southern customs and insane behaviors but it was one of my crew's never ending gas. From the moment the plane touched down on European soil, this crewmember was eating sausages and drinking beer. This diet caused one of the worst cases of flatulence (in my opinion) in human medical history. Over the years, the band has built up a tolerance for the deadly gas but this primp Englishman had not.

After days of drunken debauchery and sausage eating, the English tour manager retreated to the front of the bus. He slept sitting up, encased in his leather armor. He must have been scared to sleep in the bunks and could not stand the smell. Mr. Gasman came out of nowhere and swaggered up to the front of the bus. He got extremely close to the Englishman and then let his ass rip. Experts would describe it as 'silent but deadly' but here in the south we call it 'crop dusting'. Immediately awakened, the Englishman jumped up and yelled in a voice that could have come from the Queen of England herself, "*MY GOD!*" He started gagging and flapping his hands in front of his mouth, "*Someone's passed gas agaaaaaain!*" The gay English tour manager started to have a panic attack. At the next truck stop, he informed us that we could not work together any longer and he vanished into the English countryside. If you're reading this, sorry old chap.

CHAPTER TWO

THE BAND AND ROAD CREW STORIES

Warning! Sexual stuff. The next few tales chronicle some extreme sexual dysfunctions. You just can't make this shit up!

<> <> <>

A Different Type of Rubber

Back in the '80's, people weren't spoiled by the internet like they are today. If you wanted porn, you had to go into the stores and buy it and take it home in a brown bag. I was on the road once with a guy who was addicted to porn. He had a bag filled with porn magazines, VHS tapes of porn, various lotions and liquids and "jizz rags". Sorry to say that but it's true. The guy was thumbing through one of his porn magazines and came across an ad for penis enlargement. The ad promised "6 inches in 6 days for $6". The dumb ass actually ordered it. He talked all week long about how big his dick was going to be. The package finally arrived. He ripped open the box expecting to find a magic pill or lotion. To his disappointment, it was a rubber "extender". You simply put it on the end of your penis. Unfortunately, he was too small to even fit in the extender. But as a bonus gift, along with the extender, was a poster of porn star Jon "Wad" Holmes. The poster showed Holmes looking like he just left the set of porn film with his "member" flopping around and soaking wet. Naturally, we got a big kick out of it and hung it up in our rehearsal room. To our religious landlord's dismay, the poster was too offensive and he demanded that we take it down. He had seen a lot of weird shit but this was the straw that broke that camel's back. Earlier that week he had discovered that the penis extender dude was living in the rehearsal room without his knowledge because the guy had nowhere else to go. When I signed the lease, the landlord had two rules: 1) No one lives in the house; 2) No partying in the house. And because the rehearsal room had no running water, the guy had been pissing in Coke bottles! And that's not the most disturbing thing with this dude. One day I went over to tell the guy he couldn't stay there anymore. (Now I'm pretty hard-core but this even disturbed me.) There in the middle of the room was a strange latex head on a stand. I think it was a cosmetology head but something wasn't quite right about it. When I went to pick it up, the guy yelled, *"Stop! Don't touch that!"* I asked him why and with a sigh he said, *"Sometimes on those lonely nights when I don't get any, this is my girlfriend"*. (Y'all getting the picture here?) I yelled, *"Thanks for the warning!"* Some days I *wish* this story was made up!

<> <> <>

The Peep Show

There was another guy that I toured with that had a "bucket list". Not the kind of list of things to do before you die, but a sexual "to do" list. It was broken up into specific cities. For example, being in New York, he had no desire to see the Empire State Building or Central Park or even Madison Square Garden. This guy wanted a New York "peep show". The only way to see one of those shows was in the back of a seedy New York porn shop. But he knew that and planned out his adventure even down to his wardrobe. He bought a United States army surplus coat, logging boots that came up to his knees, leather gloves and a cowboy hat. He designed this outfit specifically to smuggle in accessories. He put a great deal of thought and effort into his plan. He talked about his plans for two months and I'm pretty sure he started planning it for over a year. His accessories included a large bottle of KY jelly, a carton of cigarettes, a gallon of whiskey and $500 in small bills. To smuggle the whiskey in, he had to tie the handle of the bottle to a leather belt under his trench coat. Alcohol was not allowed in the shows. As he finished strapping his whiskey in I asked him how long he would be. *"It could be 30 minutes or it could be 7:00 in the morning. I'll be there as long as it takes."* His plan was to get inside the show, strip completely naked, drink the entire bottle of whiskey in front of one of the girls, slather the entire bottle of KY jelly on his penis and proceed to masturbate. Unfortunately for him, he didn't get that far. There was a tollbooth at the show and the employee manning the booth was what I can only describe as a gay Frankenstein crossed with Martha Stewart! He (or she) was 6'5" tall, slicked back black hair, long painted fingernails and a dead stare. As they guy approached Mrs. Frankenstein, we watched and were sure he was going to be busted for smuggling in his accessories. Surprisingly, he was allowed in. After just a few steps, we heard what sounded like a soggy gunshot. His belt had broken and the bottle of whiskey dropped to the floor. We ran like hell! We knew that Frankenstein would have strangled us with his perfectly manicured hands. But our buddy was apprehended by Frankenstein and his life was only spared because he agreed to clean up his whiskey mess. Funny thing is, after he cleaned up the mess, they allowed him back into the peep show. He got his wish and checked it off his bucket list. Unfortunately, he had to do it sober.

<> <> <>

The Baby

This story takes place again back in the 80's. It was different then. A much simpler time and a time where we would literally "do or screw" just about anything. At that time, the band would set up in a club and play Thursday, Friday and Saturday nights and then move our asses on to the next town. One Friday night in Greensboro, North Carolina, a buddy of mine met two strippers at one of our gigs. My buddy really liked one of them and was adamant that he was going to bang her. They invited him to their place the next night but they had one condition; I had to come along to entertain the other one. Normally, I would have said hell no but back in those days, we backed each other up 'til the end. The next night after our gig, we went to their apartment. The babysitter answered the door and let us in. The girl I was supposed to be with looked a hell of a lot better the night before and much younger too. I definitely could have had sex with her but I was getting some really weird vibes so I just sat on the couch and watched TV. Fortunately before we left the gig that night, we gave the other band members the address of where we would be ... just in case they needed to search for our bodies.

My buddy and his girl were getting hot and heavy and left for the bedroom. I ended up falling asleep on the couch and woke up around 4:00 in the morning to pee. I noticed some medical equipment and pill bottles everywhere and what looked to be some sort of ventilator in the corner of the room. I thought, *"What the fuck?"* I had no idea what was going on. For all I knew they could have robbed a hospital. I crept back to the couch making sure not to wake the other girl and fell asleep again. Around 9:00 am, I woke up to a couple of my guys banging on the door. I was rescued! They were blowing the car horn and yelling for us to come on. So I jumped up and knocked on the bedroom door where my buddy was. The girl answered the door and I told her we needed to leave and to please get him up. I think she just went back to bed because we waited out in the van for him for what seemed like forever. Finally, I went back in and opened the bedroom door. I saw what seemed to be between a full size hospital bed and a crib. I tried to ignore it and yanked on my buddy's leg and told him to get up, we had to go. Seconds later, while I was waiting in the van again, my buddy comes running out of the apartment with just his jeans on and carrying the rest of his clothes. He was white as a sheet. I had never seen a look like that on his face before. He got in the van and kept saying, *"Oh my God, you're not going to believe it!"* I asked him what happened. He was trying to catch his breath and said, *"Did you see that weird bed thing in the corner of the room?"* I asked him what it was and with a shaky voice he said, *"I didn't notice it last night but when you woke me up and I was putting my shoes on I saw it. Through the medical equipment in the crib was a baby ... a full grown MAN BABY! He was wearing a diaper and had a full beard, and sat up and made a noise like 'UHHHGGGRRRRHHNNNN'!"* We all laughed our asses off and the whole band thought he was full of shit. I never saw any baby but I sure as hell saw the baby bed.

<> <> <>

The Moonlite Bunny Ranch

If you're not familiar with The Moonlite Bunny Ranch, it's a famous brothel in Nevada that was featured on HBO in the Cat House series. When we were playing Reno on an Aerosmith tour, a couple of our hyper-sexual crew had been talking about the ranch long before we arrived. When we arrived at the hotel in our bus, a couple of somewhat attractive girls approached us and gave us some $100 coupons for the bunny ranch. I knew they weren't there just for us. I think Dennis Hoff, owner of the ranch, heard Aerosmith was coming to town. (Funny now, they hung one of our platinum albums at the ranch in the summer of 2015.) The girls were probably just preying on the first bus that pulled in. At the time, most of us had girlfriends or just weren't interested. However, we had two professional perverts with us; Bucket List Man from the peep show story and my buddy from the baby story.

We handed our ranch coupons to our buddies, like we were giving them their allowance, but with a warning. *"Go get your booty but you better have your ass back here in time for load in tomorrow morning!"* Off they went and off we went to drink and gamble. The next day, the two brothel brothers were bragging about how sweet their night was. I'm not sure how much money they spent the night before, but even with the coupons, they were asking our manager for cash advances even though they had just been paid a few days before. They were bragging on their new "loves" and demanded that we give the girls all-access passes to the show. All through our sound check, they were constantly bragging on their girls. Near show time, our manager came to our dressing room and yelled at the two brothel brothers, *"Your whores have arrived!"* As usual, extreme highs gave way to extreme lows. Outside the flattering, smoky lights of the brothel, these girls looked rough. So rough that the two brothers didn't even recognize the girls. Bucket List Man said, *"That ain't the bitch I was with!"* (I'm not trying to shame anyone and Dennis, with all due respect, it was 20 years ago.) The sight of the two women in daylight shut the two men up quickly. These women were really rough looking and their new "boyfriends" could not get away from them quick enough. We got a big laugh watching the brothers try to make their escape from the girls. I guess the old saying is true, *"Bros before hoes!"*

<><><>

Healthy Competition

Back in late 90's we were at the beginning of one of our headlining tours and had a mild argument. One guy from our camp claimed he could sleep with the most unattractive and disgusting woman. Another guy from one of the opening bands claimed he could sleep with anything with a pulse. When there's a conflict like this, there's only one solution; a competition. So we pooled our money together, everyone from band members to roadies. $4,000! It would be the champion's prize. This major award aided in the competitive nature of the battle. I have to admit, the competition was a little disgusting.

Officially, it was who could fuck the ugliest woman within the 6 weeks of the tour. Judges were picked from the band and crew and the decision was verified by switching around the one-way door in the back of the bus. This was so the judges could see inside and verify what was taking place.

One night, competitor #1 brought in a girl that was very tall and looked Indian. (Not from the reservation kind of Indian but the subcontinent of India.) She wasn't unattractive enough to win the prize for the competitor, but she was a healthy start. She had a strange hairdo and looked very odd and out of place. Somehow, competitor #1 approached her and convinced her to go back to the bus with him. One of the best parts about these competitions was competitors have to constantly "one up" each other. So as a reaction to competitor #1's accomplishment, competitor #2 brought in an extremely unattractive woman ... in a wheel chair. Not only was she in a wheel chair, but the poor thing has just completed a round of chemotherapy. But she was rocked out in black leather, fish net stockings and high heels. (Note: Let me go on record by saying that ALL of these women were more than willing to participate in whatever physical activity that happened on that bus.) I was very impressed with competitor #2. This guy wanted to win so bad that he even carried the girl over his shoulder onto the bus. Afterward, we confirmed the action and competitor #2 was ahead. Not only was he ahead, but the girl actually THANKED him for the best night of her life! Competitor #1 was a bit distressed and you could see the rage in his eyes. This competition went back and forth until our very last show.

At the end of the sound check on the last day of our tour, competitor #2 was confident that he had won the battle. Competitor #1 stormed off the stage when #2 asked, *"Where the hell is he going?"* Competitor #1 approached the cleaning staff, which consisted of three very large black women, the smallest of them weighing in at about 300 pounds. I wasn't able to hear what he said to her but the middle woman laughed and touched his arm. I looked at competitor #2 and said, *"Good sir, I believe you just lost."* Competitor #1 had invited the cleaning crew to our last show that night. After a kick-ass performance, competitor #1 brought his guests back to the bus. The women were so large they had to walk sideways down the bus aisle. The soon to be champion was feeding these women drink after drink. And like clockwork, he leaned over to the largest woman and whispered something, most likely perverted, into her ear. The two made their way to the back of the bus. All during that night I had a feeling something wasn't quite right about that woman. Her feet were enormous, probably a size 15, and I noticed a 5:00 shadow growing on her face. Once the pair had gotten to the back of the bus, I looked through the reverse peephole and saw what was *supposed* to be the woman sitting on the couch. I saw the competitor's boots and his pants around his ankles. Suddenly I noticed two huge claws (or hands) grab the competitor's ass cheeks and proceeded to perform the most aggressive fellatio I had ever seen in my life.

That moment right there sealed his victory. He had his dick sucked by an enormous transsexual. He had won but he had also lost. He acted very strangely for the rest of the night and it was the last time I ever saw him.

<> <> <>

Breaking the Law! Breaking the Law!

FBI

So sometime back in the '90's, our booking agent called and said he had received a call from a promoter who had spoken with the owner of the Hard Rock Cafe in Washington, DC. The owner wanted to book *Jackyl*. Now to set the record straight, he wanted *Jackyl* because of our song "Lumberjack" and our expertise with a chainsaw. And here's why; The Hard Rock Cafe was going to be closed for a lengthy renovation so our job was to get Jesse to cut down the piano that was hanging above the main bar. The plan was for the piano to fall then would come explosions and pyrotechnics and it would be an awesome spectacle. Not to mention, it would scare the hell out of the local media covering the event, only adding to our legendary status of being rock n roll's new trouble makers. It would be a hell of a payday too, so we headed for DC.

The next morning, after riding all night on the bus, I looked out the window to see where we were. We were parked right in front of the Hard Rock Cafe in downtown Washington. Our road manager said, *"Check this out. Look across the street. That's Ford's Theater where President Lincoln was killed."* I said, *"Wow, I've always wanted to go there."* He told me, *"Well, you have two options. You can go there or take a free tour of the FBI building."* *"Where the hell is that?"* I asked. He pointed down the block and there it was. The ominous Federal Bureau of Investigation Headquarters staring me right in the face. Being on a rock 'n roll tour bus that close to the FBI made me nervous. Not that we had anything to worry about but with one push of a button, those FBI guys would know more about you than your own mama.

Our road manager told us, *"So, the owner of the Hard Rock has a brother who's an FBI agent. He could get us a special tour."* I said, *"Hell yeah, I'm in!"* This started my first adventure of the capital of the United States. So off we go across the street to FBI Headquarters where two agents were standing there waiting for us. The agents were really cool and hooked us all up, including sound guys and some roadies, with passes and a tour. We walked in the front door and joined a tour that had just started. There were probably 20 tourists and us being guided around by one of the agents, who was telling the history of the FBI. Near the end of the tour, we ended up at a gun range, which was set up like a movie theater. We were able to watch the agents fire several rounds and basically show us how badass they were.

As we were winding things up and being shown to the exit, a really hot female agent comes out of nowhere and leans between me and our road manager and says, *"Let everyone head out. Y'all just stay put."* I thought, *"Is this going to turn into some strange DC porn?"* When the tour ended, the lady agent guided us through a hidden door. I say hidden because I didn't see it before. Behind the door was an elevator, which we all got in without question. She hit some buttons and turned a special key which shot the elevator down into the ground. I'm serious when I say we must have gone down more than 10 stories. When the doors opened, we saw dozens of technicians in laboratories doing crime analysis or something that looked like it. We also saw a library that held every single gun used in a federal crime ... ever! There were guns as far as the eye could see. They showed us John Dillinger's Thompson sub machine gun and his death mask. If you're not familiar with that, during the 1920's and '30's the FBI used to make plaster molds of faces after they killed someone. And I actually TOUCHED Dillinger's death mask! After that strange but amazing part of the tour, they took us to another shooting range. This one was the actual range where agents trained. It was shot all to hell. They brought out MP5's and Sig Sauer pistols with a shit load of ammunition. Not knowing what was going on, one of the agents said, *"Thought you boys might want to do some shooting. Who's first?"* With a huge grin on my face, I stepped forward. The first thing I shot was the pistol, which wasn't a big deal since I've been a handgun owner most of my life. But, I have to admit, when an agent handed me the MP5, I was a little intimidated. And what really put me over the edge was when the agent told me, *"I have two 30 round clips for you. One is to get the feel and the other is all yours."* The agent showed me the selector switch for semi automatic. I shot a few times just to get the feel of it. At that point, I had one and a half magazines left so I went to full auto. The FBI agent stood behind me to watch the gun rising because of the possibility of recoil. He told me, half jokingly, *"Don't shoot my damn ceiling up."* We grinned at each other and I let that bad boy go. All of the bullets were gone before I knew it. I had to slap the other magazine in and let all 30 rounds go. I admit, it gave me a boner. After we finished shooting, we thanked them for that once in a lifetime experience. In return, they asked us for one favor. They wanted us to do a photo shoot for their anti drug campaign. We immediately said yes and even wore the anti drug t-shirts in the photo. We all thought that was pretty funny ... *Jackyl* on an anti-drug campaign.

Afterward, we all shook hands and they took us to the front door. As I left the building the last thing I saw was the impressive official FBI crest on the floor at the main entrance. A mere 100 feet away from the FBI headquarters, one of the roadies says, *"Hey, check it out."* and pulls out a quarter ounce of weed from his front pocket! *"I forgot I had this."* I looked at him and said , *"You fucking idiot!"* That dumb ass had infiltrated the core of the American justice system with weed. Now I know it's true and that proved it ... America is built on being hidden in plain sight.

<> <> <>

The Constant Kansas City Heart Attack

This is a double horror story. In 1995 (pre 9/11), we were in Kansas City opening for Aerosmith. We left the next day for Los Angeles to open for Bon Jovi at a RIP Magazine party. Back in the '80's and '90's, RIP Magazine was *THE* music magazine. Everyone read it. It was a big deal then. The magazine's editor, Lonn Friend, also associate editor of Hustler Magazine, personally asked us to come to the party. So we decided to fly to LA and our bus would meet us there. I threw some clothes in a bag and jumped off the bus and headed to the airport. I had forgotten I had my Beretta 9MM pistol with me. But it was no big deal. The ammo would be checked in one bag and my locked gun would be checked in another. You have to go to a specific counter to check guns so not wanting to screw things up for us, I went to the counter and had everything checked properly. I gave the ammo and magazine to Jesse to check in his bag and told him exactly what to do. After I checked the gun in, I see a half-sleepy Jesse James Dupree talking on the phone, walking straight through security. He had forgotten about checking the ammo and magazine and his bag had already reached the point of no return. One of the security officers was telling us what a great show we had done the night before. Just then, all hell broke loose.

Security swarmed around us and the shit hit the fan! Although the security officers and the cops quickly figured out it was a mistake, it was protocol for the FBI to be involved. The officers brought us over to a special room and sat us down to talk. I could hear them discussing what they should do with us. Eventually, they said they would have to take me and Jesse to the airport police station. They asked for our ID's to run through their system.

As I reached for my ID in my back pocket, I remembered a fan from the night before had put two joints in my pocket. I panicked. I just knew I was fucked. But I managed to get my wallet out of my pocket without exposing the weed. Luckily, there was one of the last remaining phone booths in the country right behind me. I managed to slip one of the joints in the coin return slot just as the officers returned. But I still had the other one.

They didn't cuff us but put us in a police car. This allowed me to shove the other joint into the crease of the seat. I pushed it in as far as it would go and prayed we would be cleared before anyone found it. When we stopped at the police station, the officer opened the door for me and I got out and the seat popped! The joint actually flipped out of its hiding place right onto the seat. You could spot it from a mile away. I was sweating bullets. By some miracle, the officer never saw it.

We went inside the station where we waited on the FBI for four fucking hours. During that time, we took pictures and signed autographs with the cops. That part was pretty cool. When the FBI finally showed up, the two agents looked like they were straight out of "Men In Black". The cops explained everything to them and they took our ID's and my gun. After a few minutes of awkward silence, one of the agents said, *"Your gun is going to have to stay at this police station for about two months while we run it through the system. You can get it back after that."* It took the FBI four hours to get there and five minutes to clear us. Fortunately, the arresting officer was a fan of the band and said he wanted to make sure I got my gun back. So he took the grips off and engraved his initials and my initials into the gun so it could be identified. I still have the pistol today and those initials are still there. The cop said, *"I'll give you boys a ride back to the terminal."* I remembered the joint was still on the seat of the police car. The terror continued. The cop opened the door for me and I still have no idea how he didn't see that bone white joint on the black leather seat. I quickly grabbed it and put it back in my pocket. We got back to the terminal and the cop was determined to escort us through security back to the same phone booth where the rest of the band was. I could see that first joint STILL sticking out of the coin slot. I walked by quickly and grabbed it and put that shit in my pocket. We got our tickets and finally got on the plane. I thought I was in the clear when I see the cop that engraved his initials into my gun standing at the cockpit. I thought they must have seen me on security cameras taking that joint out of the coin slot. That cop came over and looks right at me. I just KNEW my luck had run out. He reached into his pocket and said, *"Hey, Jeff, I forgot to give you your knife back."* When they took my gun they had also taken my knives. Holy fuck. By now, I think I shit on myself at least three or four times. At last, we were on our way and flew out to LA. When we were firmly on the ground, I smoked those two shitty little joints to the bone! It was a constant 5 hour Kansas City heart attack, but I survived.

<> <> <>

Chinatown

Any fan of *Jackyl* knows the song "Chinatown", which was on our second album *PUSH COMES TO SHOVE*. If you go back and listen to the lyrics, the following actions actually inspired that beautiful melody.

Just before we recorded our first record, we were in Boston playing some clubs. It was our first time in Boston so we did some sightseeing. Not the historic kind, oh no. We asked around and someone suggested we start in Chinatown, so off we went. We were in a certain section of Chinatown where there was every type of sex shop you could imagine. It had everything from regular porn shops to peep shows to strip clubs. It was a paradise for perverts. One of *our* perverts who was in the group was interested in a certain shop and told us to go on without him. Gladly. So we did. A little while later as we returned to our van, we came to a corner where I saw a black prostitute leaning on a car that was parked in the street. Suddenly, the car peels out and the prostitute's purse was caught on the car door handle and it dragged her down the street. My analogy was the driver of the car must have realized the prostitute was a he, not a she and booked it. When the prostitute fell, her (or his) wig came flying off. We laughed our asses off. I looked around and suddenly noticed there were more of them (prostitutes/transvestites) than there were of us. Our lingering pervert that had stayed behind, walked right into the wrong place at the wrong time. He walked right by the scene, not really paying attention, as I yelled for him to hurry the hell up. The prostitute must have thought the perv was yelling at her (or him) so he whacked him over the head with an umbrella. This man-lady of the night was built. He was at least 6 feet tall and could have been a line backer. My friend fell like a pile of bricks when the umbrella hit him and the umbrella broke his glasses. One of our road crew ran over and *decked* the prostitute in the jaw. What was once one lone prostitute turned into a street gang of trannies! They mobbed together so we took off running as fast as we could to our van. Tom was pissed. With his broken glasses he said in a low tone, " *Circle the block.*" He grabbed an empty liquor bottle and was ready to throw it when I yelled, *"Let's get the hell out of here. We're not circling no block!"* As we were driving away, another band member grabbed an orange squirt gun that we had bought at a novelty shop, South of the Border. He yelled out the window, *"I don't know what you're*

packing but I know what I'm packing!" Then we noticed a car
with the lights off was following us. Then another car started
tailing, then another. I yelled, *"Oh shit!"* There were 4 or 5 cop
cars following us and as soon as I yelled, the blue lights and sirens
started up. We pulled over immediately. Those Boston cops
weren't fucking around. At gunpoint, they grabbed Jesse and one
of the roadies out of the front of the van. They shined lights into
the back of the van and then dragged us all out. We were put face
down on the street. They searched the van and found a weed
pipe, a film canister with a very small bud of marijuana in it and
our main weapons ... two orange squirt guns. Two cops wearing
suits got out of an unmarked car and looked extremely puzzled.
My guess was they were either lieutenants or detectives and
probably in charge. I watched them talk to the arresting officers.
They looked over at our Georgia license plate then back over at
our dumb asses on the ground. They stood us all up and asked us
who was leading the group. Jesse and I raised our hands and
simultaneously said *"I guess we are."* One of them pointed at Jesse
and said, *"Well, I pick you. What's your business here in Boston?"*
Jesse explained to him that we were in a band from the South and
it was our first time in Boston. In my dumb ass southern accent I
said, *"We wanted to see the sights."*

    The guy shouted back, *"Don't you know you'll get yourselves
killed fucking around in Chinatown at night?"* Then they took
Jesse and me to one of the cars. The squirt guns, weed pipe and
weed were on the hood of the car. One of the cops told Jesse to
pick up the pipe and weed. He had already told the police the
weed wasn't Jesse's and one of the road crew had claimed it. I
tried to protest but the cop looked dead into my eyes and said,
"Was I talking to you?" That cop was 100 % no bullshit. Jesse
looked over at me and said, *"Bail me out."* He thought they were
pinning it on him and he was going to jail. Jesse picked up the
pipe and the weed and the no bullshit cop said, *"Throw it in the
water."* To our amazement, we were pulled over right next to the

Boston Harbor. As fate would have it, we were looking straight at the famous Boston Tea Party Ship from the Revolutionary War! I couldn't believe it. I could see the silhouette of the ship in the night's sky. Jesse threw that shit right underneath the ship. It was amazing. That act alone was awesome. It was an incredible symbol. It was perfect. The cop made all of our crew guys throw the squirt guns in the trash can. The other suited cop yelled at the others to get back in the van. Then he looked at me and Jesse and said, *"If I see any of you or this piece of shit van back here again I will take you all to jail for threatening people with a gun. Get your country asses to your hotel immediately!."* We all said *YES SIR* and tried to get the hell out of there. The only problem was the cops had blocked us in so Jesse had to do a 7 point turn to get going. Just before we left, Jesse asked the cop *"Umm sir, how do we get to our hotel?"* The cop yelled the directions into the van and we were gone. The funny part of this story was that The Boston Tea Party was originally about fighting against government tyranny. So our act of throwing the weed under the ship was the same act of freedom. We were the *rock* version of the Sons of Liberty!

< > < > < >

My Favorite Sherpa

Over the years, *Jackyl* has had its fair share of some real characters eager to work on our road crew. I've known a lot of distinct people during my career but there's this one guy that really stands out. On this guy's first day at work with us, he shows up dressed like a Himalayan Sherpa. Keep in mind; he was from Dallas, Georgia, not Texas or even the Himalayas. He was wearing hardcore sandals/work boots, an embroidered vest and linen pants. *Jackyl* does not have a strict dress code, but come the fuck on. No one will be walking off of our tour bus dressed like a damn Sherpa! We could fix his clothing if he was a good worker. But his real problem was his mouth. This Sherpa told us not only could he out drink us, he could drink $300 worth of Jagermeister. Once again, the situation turned into a contest.

Now, I want to make one thing clear, we didn't challenge him, he challenged us. I looked over at my buddy Roman and asked him how much cash he had on him. He said, *"I've got $200 to $300 to spend. What do you have?"* With an evil smile I said, *"I've got the same."* One of the first shows Mr. Sherpa worked on with us was the Harley Davidson 100 Year Anniversary show held in Milwaukee, Wisconsin, which was also a Full Throttle event. Let me say, this show was HUGE! The stage was inside a NASCAR track with vendors set up in a ring around the crowd.

The first night, we made our way through the crowd to the Full Throttle tent, dragging the Sherpa with us. Within two hours, we had given him about $450 worth of Jager.

The Sherpa man was dancing all over the tent and kicking his feet in the air. It was hilarious. He climbed on top of one of the bars and continued to dance his ass off. Full Throttle security told me and Roman to get him off the bar. I reached up and grabbed him by the back pocket and pulled. At the time, I was unaware that his pants had dry-rotted so when I pulled, it tore the entire left side of his pants completely off. Here was the drunk Sherpa, dancing on top of a speaker with his balls hanging out, with about 3,000 people watching him. He refused to get down and at that point, Roman tried to set what was left of his pants on fire. The cops came up and said, *"You can't do that."* The Sherpa jumped down yelling at the cops, *"They can set me on fire if they want to!"* He ran off and disappeared into the crowd. We continued to party a little bit longer, not really knowing or caring where the Sherpa was. Then the DJ called, *"Last call for drinks."* and he put on our song The Lumberjack. Normally, I hate it when they play our songs because I play them all the time. But that night it was the perfect song to play. As the song kicked in, I heard a woman scream. The crowd parted and here comes the Sherpa. With dick, balls and all, he was carrying a chair above his head. He was imitating Jesse playing The Lumberjack on stage. At this point, the cops returned and told us we needed to get his ass out of there. Most of the cops were laughing but one of them was not amused. To add to the chaos, a big storm was coming through. We all piled into a van, loaded the drunken Sherpa and headed to the apartments where we were staying. It just so happened these apartments were located on a very nice golf course. As soon as the van stopped, the Sherpa jumped out and started to run onto the golf course. Roman went into hot pursuit after him. As lightening streaked through the air, you could see Roman fighting the Sherpa in the pouring rain. This was a pretty strong thunderstorm with hail and all.

I gave the Sherpa and Roman one last chance to come in and then I went to bed. I woke up the next morning and one of our road crew said, *"You better go check on that Sherpa."* I go in another room and see a body in a bed. It's completely covered in a sheet except for two big, dirty feet. In his long, disgusting toenails were chunks of sod and grass. Hoping he's not dead, I pulled one of his legs. He sat up and said, *"What the hell happened to me?"* Roman walked into the room and said, *"Congratulations mother fucker, you did it! You drank $450 worth of Jager."* The Sherpa looked at us with the most bloodshot eyes I had ever seen. They looked as if he were going to bleed to death through his eyeballs. *"Where's my clothes?"* he asked. I said, *"Dude, you were lucky. You lost that Sherpa getup last night."* He said, *"But I have nothing to put on."* I shouted, *"You mean that's all the clothes you had?"* *"Yep,"* he said. My brother, who had been watching the whole thing, said, *"You mean you don't have ANY clothes?"* He said that was all he had. So off we went to the cheapest place we could find to shop for the Sherpa ... Sears. That day there was a big sale so we bought him some pants, a shirt and socks for $16. Within a week, the Sherpa said he couldn't take it and was gone. It was one of the greatest nights of my life. That was my favorite Sherpa. For two days after that, my jaw hurt from laughing so much. *Jackyl* is a very charitable band: Why?

Jagermeister - $ 450

Sears Clothing - $ 16

$450 + $16 + One missing Sherpa = Priceless

<><><>

Odd Jobs

Odd jobs are primarily reserved for crewmembers but back in the day when we were all broke, everyone did them. An "odd job" is any crazy, stupid act that someone would perform for the money in someone's pocket or a set amount of funds raised. It was like a fucked up lottery. For example, wearing chaps without underwear (penis fully exposed) and walking through a hotel lobby and across a highway would be considered an odd job. Or having to eat a bun that was jammed in a band member's ass would be considered an odd job. Now that the band members don't really need the money, the odd jobs have been placed on the road crew. Rumor had it that Metallica raised a large sum of money for any crewmember who could get a picture of themselves eating the pussy of the ugliest girl they could find. Now I don't know if this is actually true, but if it is it's fucking awesome. That's a pretty decent odd job but our problem was that our road crew did that shit for fun in their free time. Our odd jobs could start small but would go through some fucked up evolution when additional band members became interested. For instance, Roman would tell a crewmember he would give them $100 to "eat that", whatever *that* may be. He would then ask me to pitch in. At that point, the stakes were high at $200. Then Jesse pitched in another $300.

With the extra money, the condition was you had to eat it PLUS you had to do it butt ass naked! So there we were, rolling down the highway in the bus with a crewmember eating a disgusting concoction butt-ass naked. Needless to say, that lucky gentleman made $500. Now you can see why they're called "odd jobs". But with that kind of money, it was a *bonafide* job!

<><><>

The Yule Log

Fans are constantly bringing us gifts of all kinds. Sometimes it's liquor, sometimes it's some kinds of clothing. We never know what will be next. For some reason, especially around the holidays, we get tons of food. We've had Thanksgiving turkeys in Texas, lobster in Massachusetts, and an enchilada dinner made by someone's grandmother in New Mexico. During recent Christmas holidays, we received a 2 foot by 3 foot platter filled with exactly 100 cookies. They were not store bought cookies. They were huge individually decorated cookies covered in gobs of multicolored icing with a powdering of sprinkles on top. They were perfectly separated into two equal portions as if it were destiny. Eating contest!

The cookies arrived around 3:00 PM and by 4:00 PM, we had two competitors and a $400 pot. The two competitors were almost at blows at the time of the contest because we had worked them up so hard. I'm known to be the king instigator of the group with my brother, Roman Glick, a close second to the throne.

We had been talking this damn contest up all day. It was the super bowl of stupidity. Teams had been chosen and bets had been placed. No one wanted to look like a loser in front of us and it started to get ugly. There was only one request from each competitor. Each wanted their own gallon of whole milk. In the world of rock 'n roll, that took all of five seconds to get. Both competitors had their different strategies; one was tearing right through all of the cookies as fast as possible, the other had decided that slow and steady wins the race. This was truly the tortoise and the hare and the game was afoot.

Roadie #1 (the hare), with his fast as possible strategy, was on his 18th cookie when Roadie #2 (the tortoise) was only on his 5th. Around cookie #20, the hare's face contorted and his eyes seemed to melt. He sat back. Now I've seen people trip on a number of drug and alcohol combinations in my day but this man was really tripping ... on Christmas cookies. Yep, some beautifully decorated cookies made from love turned a man from Dr. Jekyll to Mr. Hyde. With every cookie after #20, it was like he was transforming into a fucking werewolf! He started to get really pissed too. When we talked trash to him, he would only respond with *"Fuck you mother fuckers! You think this shit is funny?"* Well yes, we do. Then he leaned forward and put his head down. At that point, we thought the slow and steady strategy was actually going to work. The tortoise was as relaxed as he could be, dunking his cookies in cold milk and laughing his ass off at the now violently ill (and pissed off) hare. But things changed as soon as the tortoise hit the 20th cookie mark. He had to stop. He had that same transforming look in his eyes and said, *"Damn, dawg. Too much fucking sugar."* He started to feel the pain and they both needed a break. Plus, they were really pissed. I told them they had a time limit and they said, *"Bullshit!"* Jesse piped in and said, *"If you mother fuckers drag this out I am going to pull my money out."* I told the two competitors they had one more hour to finish plus they had to hold it down for an hour. Now with the time limit, the two very angry men rallied and continued. The tortoise took five more cookies and said, *"That's it. This isn't worth the money. My life is worth more. I'm out!"* The tortoise quit around cookie #24. The hare was behind at that point by only six cookies. Those last six cookies may as well have been a mountain. These guys were really struggling. The tortoise got up and went to the bathroom. (*Note: Being on a tour bus is like being on a cruise ship. You are constantly being tossed around like a boat on the water.) When the tortoise went to the bathroom, he was being rocked around and finally puked. At that point, he was officially disqualified. Roadie #1 said, *"I knew I would win! Watch this!"* He had already won but wanted to beat Roadie #2's number. He only needed to eat two more cookies. Hence, man's downfall is his pride. In his head, he had to beat the other roadie by four cookies. After he had won and had the cash in hand, there was no celebration. He could only roll around in his chair and make strange noises. That was around 3:00 in the morning. At 9:00 the next morning, the bus stopped at a truck stop. I got off the bus to get a cup of coffee and use the bathroom. The hare also got off the bus but after awhile, he was nowhere to be found. I heard screams coming from the bathroom so I ran in to see what was going on. He had just given birth to a massive shit. It was the exact size and color of a Christmas Yule log. You could even see the multicolored sprinkles he had swallowed whole. The hare looked at me and said he was done. *"I'm going home. I can't do it anymore. The things that you all do are insane. I love you guys like brothers but I'm out."* That's the story of how Christmas cookies broke a man.

<> <> <>

The Bear Sausage

This story is about the second time we thought we would lose a man. Not to drugs or alcohol, but to food. This was about a guy we liked to call The Handyman. He's a stocky Norwegian that can eat a massive amount of just about anything, or so he thought.

We were finishing up our show at Sturgis one year when a fan who was a hunter from Canada, gave us a large assortment of meats. We got everything from different types of jerky to one large bear sausage. The bear sausage was the girth of a man's arm and has a dark brown color. We had plenty of time, disposable income and weird food. That meant an "odd job" was on the way.

The Handyman had heard about the Christmas cookie incident and said for the money, he would do anything. I have personally seen him eat 11 little Krystal burgers, 3 regular sized Krystal double cheeseburgers, 4 orders of fries, 3 large sweet teas and a jar of mayonnaise herring, all in one sitting. He told us, *"Y'all ain't shit. I can handle anything."*

Back at the house we rented in Sturgis, Roman Glick and I started to put the odd job together. We found a huge bag of frozen pancakes, some peanut butter, Karo syrup and some butter and of course, the bear sausage. Chef Roman started to work on the concoction. The Handyman's only request was to have everything heated. *"Sure, anything for you sir."* I said. I microwaved the pancakes and Roman cut the sausage into one inch pieces and sautéed them in butter. The order was one pancake slathered in butter, covered in peanut butter and bear sausage on top. This was repeated 10 times. To finish it off, it was all drenched in Karo syrup. If you don't know, Karo syrup is a really thick, harsh corn syrup that's mostly used for cooking. We dubbed the creation "The Cake".

I don't recall how much money was involved but it was low, maybe $200. It didn't draw much of a crowd or spectators, but the Handyman tore into it anyway. When I say he can eat anything, I mean he can eat ANYTHING. Especially after smoking a half bag of weed. I shit you not. After about 45 minutes, he had eaten the foot and a half tall cake. However, the extreme amount of food and the gamey iron taste of the bear sausage was just too much. But he kept it down. The one thing that really screwed him over was that he had to keep it down for an hour. What he didn't know was that we had to board a private plane in an hour and it was a thirty minute ride to the airport.

During the drive to the airport, he began screaming, gagging and moaning. Although he wasn't mad at us, every time he gagged he looked at us like it was our fault. It was like he was giving birth and blaming the husband and yelling, *"You did this to me!"* Hey, it takes two to tango. We finally arrived at the airport and Roman was watching him like a hawk. Roman told the Handyman, *"If I see one drop of puke, you're out!"*

We started to load the plane while the Handyman was gagging violently underneath the plane. He looked as if he was close to death and all I could do was laugh. He took the devil's deal. It was his choice but he did make the $200. I might have presented the odd job to him but then again, that's why I'm called The Instigator. It was like the Seinfeld episode where Jerry is listening to George complain and Jerry says, *"Your pain is my pleasure."* Genius!

<> <> <>

The Power of One Drink

The Handyman is an interesting gentleman and we know how much he can eat. He can also drink as much as he can eat. Once, I fed him 48 shots of liquor. I swear to God! I was playing with a friend of mine at a local bar with my punk rock side band called Super V. It was Handyman's job to be my designated driver that night so I let him drive my Mercedes to the bar. I paid him $100 plus all the food he could eat. It was normal for him to sit in the car for four hours and eat. But that night he went inside the bar. The opening band was playing and I told Handyman that I would buy him one drink, but that was it. He wasn't sure what he wanted to drink so he left it up to me. That was his first mistake.

First, I asked my brother if I could ride home with him. He said yes so Handyman's fate was sealed. I went to the bar and ordered what I call a layered shot. I told the bartender, in these exact words, *"I would like a tall glass with a shot of the cheapest tequila you have, followed by peppermint schnapps, then Bacardi 151 and top it off with the Greek liquor, Ouzo."* By the time I made it to Handyman's table, the drink had separated into four layers. He looked at me and said, *"What the hell is that!"* I told him he better drink it because I paid for it. Cheers! He threw the drink back without coughing or gagging. He kept a straight face for a few seconds and then stared right at me like I had done something bad to him. At that point the opening band had finished their first song so I jumped up on stage and yelled, *"It's Handyman's birthday!"* But it wasn't. People started buying him drinks of every kind. I told them to get him the most fucked up drink imaginable. The liquor started flowing like water. I knew he had 48 shots because I covered all the drinks for the house that night and told the bartender to put them all on my tab so I could keep count.

Later that night after we played, I couldn't find Handyman. I asked around and some girl said there was a guy out back "hollerin". We drove my brother's truck around to the back of the bar and turned on the head lights. We called his name and heard a terrible grunt. There he was, down at the bottom of a mud pit. If he had fallen a few more feet in the other direction, he would have drowned in a pond. I retraced his footsteps and found him stuck in the mud. He had fallen, end over end, and somehow landed straight up on his feet. He was completely covered in mud. We pulled him out and threw him in the back of the truck and drove away.

About halfway home, Handyman started standing up in the back of the truck, like a scene from Titanic. We told him to sit his ass down because the highway patrol was known to stake out that road. I knew if they saw him the cops would take us all to jail. I told him I would personally beat his ass if he didn't get down.

Once we got home, I stripped him down to only his underwear and hosed him off. There was no way I was going to let him in my house so I took him to my recording studio next door. My buddy, Jack Warren, agreed to sit and watch him, like a sick child. The last thing I saw before I went to bed that night was Handyman crawling around on the deck of the recording studio puking his guts out.

The next morning there was a knock at the door. It was Handyman. I had completely forgotten about his drunken ass. He looked like he had been hit in the face with a shovel. His eyes were so fucking blood shot. Remember, he's Norwegian. He's just as round as he is tall. Somehow, he had managed to get his pants back on but the legs were so long, he was using the bottom of them as shoes since he had lost his shoes the night before. He asked me what had happened to him. I told him the truth. *"You partied your ass off!"* He said, *"Please help me."* I had a pot of old coffee that I microwaved and gave it to him along with a loaf of bread and a bottle of Pepto-Bismol, which he put in his coffee as creamer. He sipped some coffee and put slices of bread on his face. I have no idea why he did that.

Under protest, my buddy Jack drove him home and I didn't see the Handyman again for three weeks. When he did call me he said, *"I crawled into the tub and laid there for three days. I had blood coming out of my ass and penis! You should open a rehab clinic because Alcoholics Anonymous don't have shit on you!"* He said he was never going to drink again. He may be on to something there.

CHAPTER THREE

ROAD MEDICINE

<><><>

The Free Clinic

When we first started out, *Jackyl* played a club in Myrtle Beach, South Carolina called Rock Burgers. During the summer, this was the place to be. We would play three 45 minute sets every night except Sundays. We started our first set around midnight, which was perfect because that's when the strip clubs and bars were closing and Rock Burgers would be filling up.

One of the guys in our crew had the ability to lay Miss America at the drop of a hat with no problem. Instead, he liked to scrape the bottom of the barrel. We're all God's children but come on. As an analogy, instead of eating at a five star restaurant, he would rather pick through the dumpster behind the bar.

One Friday night before we played, this guy showed up with a female carnival worker. (I can't make this stuff up.) This chick was disgusting. She hadn't had a shower in a week and didn't even own shoes. We all warned him not to but he did her anyway, for the next three days. After we left town, we ragged on him about it but his reply was always, *"Fuck y'all. That was some good pussy!"* A few days later, Mr. Fuck Y'all called me into a bathroom with a very concerned look on his face. He pulled his jeans and underwear down to his ankles. While he was doing this, the head of his penis was STUCK to his underwear with a glue-like substance that had a yellow discharge. I knew exactly what it was. I yelled and pointed at his diseased member, *"Dude, that's Chlamydia!"* He started to panic and didn't know what to do. We were all broke at the time so I told him to go to a free clinic.

He wanted me to go with him, like he was a four year old. I said, *"Hell no!"*. He got into our yellow school bus and started to circle the hotel where we were staying. With every pass, he would flip me off and yell about how bad a friend I was. After the third pass, he sped off. In his haste and anger, he took off without directions to the clinic.

<> <> <>

The Curing of the Crabs

The same fella that had to take his antibiotics for Chlamydia had come down with the worst case of crabs I had ever seen. During that time we were broke as hell so I served as the resident doctor and stylist. For example a week earlier I gave this same guy a homemade perm. Apparently I did something wrong. The directions said to leave it in for 45 minutes but being poor at that time, I thought if you left it in for 2 hours, it would last twice as long. This made half of his hair fall out, leaving the other half of his hair looking like it had been 'set' like someone's grandmother. But once again, this guy screwed around with the wrong chick and got crabs. I had heard the wise advice of soaking the infested area with bleach. I had no idea you were supposed to water down the bleach. Before the chemical attack on the crabs, we made the guy shave his body from neck to toes and then we laid him down in the bath tub. I started pouring five gallons of bleach onto his naked body. He instantly started to complain that it burned but he was determined to get rid of those crabs. Keep in mind, he was 100% sober during this crab killing. He stayed in the bath tub for about four hours and said, *"That's it!"* He got out of the tub and walked into the room where the rest of us were. His entire body looked like he was severely sunburned. His skin was dark pink, scaling and peeling. He said his eyes and head were itching like hell. To top it off, the crabs had invaded the back of his head, his eye lashes and his eye brows. The only thing the crabs did was move up to the east side! I soon found out that you don't use bleach on crabs, you use something called Rid-Ex, which could be bought in a drug store. The funniest thing about this story is that in the store in Myrtle Beach, SC, hanging above the right crab cream was a plastic blow up crab for kids to play with in a swimming pool!

<><><>

The Foot Flap (The Flesh Flip Flop)

This next story is short but extremely gross. At one point on a tour, one of our crewmembers had a slight foot issue. It was around April when I noticed a large callus on this guy's foot. I told him, *"Dude, you better get that looked at."* July came around and the next couple of months he did nothing about the callus. It had turned into what I called "The Foot Flap". Let me explain. One morning I woke up to hear him whimpering in the back of the bus so I went back to investigate. I opened the door and the first thing that hit me was the stench. I'll never forget the smell of that rotten foot. The callus had grown from the base of his toes to the back of his heel. Close to his in-step, the callus had split, revealing inflamed skin. He was literally wearing a flesh foot flop! It had been so painful that he even tried to duct tape the callus back on. At this point, there was nothing Dr. Jeff could do for him. We had to get him a plane ticket back home to have his foot medically shaved. The moral of this story is there was no road medicine for this man. He couldn't be saved ... and he had to pay for his own plane ticket home.

CHAPTER FOUR

PLANES, VANS, CARS & BUSES

From my career on the road, I could write an entire book on the vehicles that took us touring around the world. What are now tour buses and airplanes use to be vans and cars. Our first chariot was actually a retired yellow school bus, and that brings us to our first story.

<> <> <>

The Short Bus

Right out of high school I started to book our first shows. Within a year we had built up a fan base that extended outside of my local area. Because of that, we needed some form of transportation to take the band and our gear on the road. I talked to my dad about our needs and he passed the word along to his drinking buddies. It wasn't long until one of his friends got back to us with an old short yellow school bus he had for sale at his junk yard. Yes, the same kind of bus you see used to transport mentally challenged children to and from school. It was the perfect ride for us! We immediately went to work making it into the perfect tour bus. We left the first two rows of seats in and built bunk beds in the back. That still left five feet in the back for gear. We were in business.

Our first gig out of town started in Fayetteville, NC about a five hour drive from my hometown. As soon as we took off we were in euphoria. We were partying our asses off but as soon as we got to the point of no return things started to come apart. We didn't anticipate one key thing. School buses are only for around town use and short distances. The first five miles of the trip we found out how fast our short bus could go. If you were going

DOWN hill with your foot to the floor you might get up to 42 mph. It was a scene straight out of Monty Python; the country version. Then we found ourselves dying. The short bus couldn't take the extreme weight of our gear and the speed we were pushing it to. Only an hour and a half from my house it started to kick like a rented mule. The engine was over heating causing the mufflers to burn out and holes started appearing in the middle of the floor board. They were literally glowing red hot. The rubber strip was melting in the middle of the aisle and fumes were choking us. I remembered my grandfather telling me you could repair the muffler with soda cans and old coat hangers. We let the thing cool off at a rest stop then bought $20 worth of sodas. After chugging the drinks we repaired the mufflers and were on the road again. After stopping about 15 times to put water in the radiator and refueling, we eventually got to the gig in Fayetteville, North Carolina. Luckily, we did not have to move it for three days, but after our third show it was time to return home. Normally it's a 5 or 6 hour drive but it took us 16 hours to get there and around 20 hours to get back. We finally limped the short bus from Hell back to my front yard, leaking fluids from every orifice possible. We drove straight back to the junk yard we bought it from. Just a few days earlier I paid $800 for this piece of shit and the same guy offered me $60 to take it back. I agreed to it immediately and got the fuck out of there. Lesson learned.

<> <> <>

The Volvo and The Station Wagon

So after the bus debacle we needed a new way to get around. My Dad's buddy's junkyard had a Volvo truck without a box on the back that he sold to us for $2500. We didn't have 25 cents to our names so we worked out a payment plan with the owner. I think he felt bad about the yellow bus, but not so much as to reduce the price. My brother Chris and I went to pick it up one night and within an hour I learned never to slam on the breaks of a truck that has no weight in the back. Driving on the way home, a car in front of us slammed on the brakes. I hit the brakes a little bit too hard. I swear to God we did a front wheelie and I could see the damn pavement right in front of my eyes. We teetered a bit on the front tires then slammed back down. I think I shit in my pants a little. We drove off like nothing happened.

I didn't eat for the next two months but I somehow found the money for a cargo box for the truck. We were in business again. Later we bought a 1982 Pontiac station wagon with bench seats. We had this combo for a few years. One night at a gig we had our back window of the station wagon busted out. Every time it rained water would pool up in the back where your feet would be. It was like a disgusting hot tub, except it wasn't hot and the water was brown. So we had this system of rotation that ensured everyone would have equal time in the shitty seat, a comfy seat or driving.

The old Pontiac station wagon was good to us until one fateful night. We were in route to Petersburg, Virginia on I-95. I smelled oil burning but that was nothing new. Then I heard the terrible sound of metal on metal grinding. The entire car started to shake from the engine back. The engine seized up on the highway. Someone had forgotten to ever change the oil so we had been running without oil for miles. If it was anything other than an American car, we would have never made it that far. In those days we always had a convoy going. Remember, this was in the days of no cell phones. We were only 25 miles to our destination. I knew at the end of the day I could scrap the station wagon for $100-$150, money that we needed. So the natural *Jackyl* instinct was to tow the broken down station wagon with the Volvo truck. The convoy started with the station wagon in front with the truck following with the equipment. Now it was the truck in front towing the station wagon with a rope. The really weird part was that everyone kept the same seats. After a bit of highway, we saw a sign that said '10 miles to Petersburg.' I thought we almost had it. Then I saw a sign that read '5 miles to Petersburg,

2 miles to weigh station.' I know you've seen weigh station signs, it either says open or closed. This one said *"You're fucked."* Every truck has to be weighed and there is no way in hell they would allow a station wagon strapped to it. So we devised a plan to unhook the station wagon from the truck and have the truck go ahead to be weighed. While they were doing that we would keep the lights on the wagon and have someone pretend like they were driving while the rest of us pushed the piece of shit down the main highway in front of the weigh station. We couldn't just push it from the back because they would see us; we all concentrated on the left side. My hope was that they thought it was just an extremely slow driver. Thinking back it's funny as hell but at the time I was scared shitless. Because it was a busy weigh station, 18 wheelers were blocking the highway patrols' view. We got about half way when a big truck pulled away, exposing us. It felt like the first time your mother catches you masturbating. We kept the act up, trying to play cool, but here they came. Two highway patrol cars approached us with their lights on. The trooper gets out and says, *"What in the hell are you doing? You can't tow that!"* I told him that our car broke down and we weren't towing it. He shined his flash light on the hood and the damn rope we were using to tow it was still tied to the bumper. He said, *"You can't tow it, you can't push down the highway, you can't walk down the highway, and you can't leave the piece of shit! What are you going to do?"* I stood there speechless, with a dumb look on my face. The trooper continued his lecture in an easier tone. *"Because you made us laugh I won't take you to jail but figure something out!"* He took me inside the weigh station and watched me call a tow truck to come get the piece of shit car. I rang up a 24/7 towing company. I swear the phone rang 25 times until some old guy who must have been asleep picked up. I told him where I was and that he can have the car if he came and got it. So I had to wait an hour with the trooper breathing down my neck. The entire time I was waiting, our

equipment truck kept going up the next exit, turning around, and getting weighed again. They repeated this until I was the last one standing. The trooper then told me that if he didn't come soon we had to go with him to the sheriff's office. So I called the towing company back and the same guy answered and said, *"Wait, you want me to come now?"* With that the trooper grabbed the phone and talked to the guy. After a quick conversation the trooper told me that the towing guy promised he was coming to take it away. He asked if I had a ride and I said, *"Yes, they'll be here in the minute."* I awkwardly shuffled outside with the trooper. While this was going on, *Jackyl* had a few tricks up their sleeves. I saw our Volvo truck pulling away from being weighed for the 50th time. I stood there in silence, waiting for that truck to pull back around. The trooper was about to say something to me but another trooper told him he had a phone call. At that time the Volvo came back and I hopped in. We started to book it out of there but my crew guy was in the truck driving. I asked him, *"Where is everybody?"* He only pointed his thumb back towards the cargo box. There were eight guys already piled into the back with the equipment. I thought we were good but once again, two marked state patrol cars started to follow us. I knew then we were fucked! But they didn't turn their lights on. They just followed us all the way to the hotel where we were staying. As soon as we got into the parking lot the cops drove past us, looked us up and down, and then drove off. We got a nice little police escort to finish our night off of shitty luck. I still to this day believe that those troopers knew exactly what was going on the whole time.

<><><>

The Orange Van

Any fan of *Jackyl* would know our first music video "I Stand Alone". That video originally cost $15,000 (that we had to beg for) but it ended up costing us around $1,015,000. (We'll talk about that a little later). If you remember in that video there was an orange van that we blew up. After the death of the Pontiac station wagon we purchased a 1983 orange Dodge"Tradesmen" van and hit the road. This van had the famous Dodge 318 V8 engine. Every single master mechanic told me that if you keep oil in that engine, it will go forever. That was true up until we blew it up in our music video. Even though Hollywood filmed it, we took it upon ourselves to blow it up. Here's why. Back in its day this was the only vehicle I've known to literally catch the crabs. Near the end of its life all of the weather stripping was gone so in the winter we had to insulate all of the windows with duct tape. Almost every single little crack had to be sealed up just leaving the driver's door and one of the windows in the back. My brother, being the smallest, jumped through the back window and then sealed it up behind him. Another thing I should mention; the passenger seat got screwed up because we were rocking back and forth on it and found out that if you twisted the seat backwards it would fit into place again. I think in our "I Stand Alone" video you can actually see the passenger seat turned around. For the video shoot, my friend Virgil, ex 82nd Air Borne Ranger and Special Forces educated, made a mixture of fertilizer and kerosene, some half sticks of dynamite and about 8 gas cans (with blasting caps). The cherry on top was he threaded a blasting cap into the gas tank. This explosive was big enough to put this van out of its misery, plus it would look great on camera!

Fast forward to the music video. Driving to the film location Jesse James Dupree had the van up to 115 mph, this is scary in itself but all of a sudden the power steering belt snapped. Thank God Jesse kept it under control and we didn't wreck or I would not be telling this story now. So when we blew up this van, we weren't wrecking a perfectly good vehicle; it was more like putting the sick family dog down. We actually blew this piece of shit up on someone's property without their permission. We didn't even know these people. We just found an open field out in the middle of nowhere. After my friend Virgil set up the explosives the cameras rolled. We jumped into the van and Virgil lit the fuse. As the cameras rolled we jumped out of the van as the explosion happened. The camera crew wrapped it up and we got the fuck out of there. As a side note, we had gotten rid of all identification on the van. We took the tags off, the VIN number on the dash, and the serial number on the engine. On way out we passed a little farmer on his way to investigate the massive explosion. We didn't stop but his facial expression was priceless. He probably thought we blew up bodies in the back of that van. I guess you're wondering why it cost $1,015,000 since we were doing our own stunts. Here's why. Immediately after filming the death of the van, we had another scene to shoot. This consisted of us going into a Longhorn Steakhouse in downtown Atlanta. Jesse was going to crank the chainsaw and saw a certain Geffen Record rep's table in half. We trusted that the video director and restaurant manager had cleared us for this stunt. I can't say much about it but it was a busy lunch that day and Jesse would appear to be a crazed chainsaw maniac. This is where the $1,000,000 of legal fees and broken knees came crashing down.

But that was a transition for us because not only did we have a record deal, we also had our record finished and we were on our way to our first big tour. Looking back on it, it was probably the best thing that happened to us. With us owing Geffen Records so much money, they had to invest in our future. We had to get rich to pay them back.

<><><>
Our First Tour Bus
Before we went on our first big tour, we got some of the best advice from John Kalodner (*note to bands) *"Do not take the 'tour support' money."* All that money is just more debt to the record company so we learned how to be self-sufficient on the road. At that point we had a gold record but our budget only allowed us an old 1981 Eagle tour bus. An Eagle was just an old Greyhound bus. This bus was ridden hard in the 80's. There was

probably semen on the ceiling from every hit band on the classic rock radio. We called it the Journey Bus after Journey the band. If you scraped the top of that bus ceiling you could easily make a rock baby with the DNA. That bus made it through decades of rock but it only took *Jackyl* two days in the winter to kill it.

Our bus driver was terrible and the power was even out on the bus. We overheard the driver call the bus company saying, "*Fuck you and fuck this bus!*" If you heard that, it meant you were screwed. We already had a new bus coming to get us but that was at our next gig that was 200 miles away. This bus driver was ready to go home right then and there. So we told our bus driver we would get all of our shit and leave only if he got us to the next gig. He wasn't having any of it. (This next moment I am going to share with you showed me that Jesse is the best singer and the best manager for *Jackyl*.) When the bus driver wouldn't drive us to the next gig, Jesse jumped out of his bunk, ran outside in the snow with no shoes or pants on, and chased this damn bus driver all around the hotel parking lot and threatened to beat his ass until he took us to the next show. The bus driver eventually got us there. Just so you know, this wasn't the last time *Jackyl* had to fight to get to a gig. We will never let anyone stop us from playing for our fans.

<><><>

The Good, The Bad, The Driver

Most high dollar busses are very comfortable. There is only one thing that can ruin a good bus and is a real issue; the driver. I have my list of favorite drivers, keep in mind this is just my list. I want to name these guys by name. Our first driver and good friend to this day is Clay McGuinness. He was the old driver for Lynyrd Skynyrd. He allegedly drove a van from each gig for Skynyrd carrying all of their goodies. All I know is that he is great driver and all around great guy. Another favorite of ours was Don Townsend. He drove for everyone from Brad Paisley to Ozzy. He was actually *Jackyl's* first sound man. He's a great friend of the band. Next up is Jeff McCardle, the smoothest bus driver ever. You could leave the gig and travel 500 miles and never know it. He introduced us to Justin Timberlake. He is also the only driver we allowed to drive 200 miles out of the way so he could pick up homemade pies from mother's house. Then we have "Bevis". He was the driver for most of our Guinness Book of World Records 100 shows in 50 days tour. And lastly we have "Shaggy", a biker, a wild crazy man, and the destroyer of the Mona Lisa**.

All of these drivers had their own personality that clicked with the band. On the road, if the driver was cool, we liked to treat them like a member of the band. If they helped us out, we would take care of them. Now there are plenty of ok drivers. But there are a select few that were the worst. You have the guys that don't even want to be there. They won't work with the band on their schedule and they fight you every step of the way. Here is an example of how bad and bizarre it can get with these drivers. We even had a driver that was sitting down with us at dinner and out of nowhere he told us he was contemplating suicide because he's divorcing his wife. Who the hell says that in front of people? Within two seconds of that, Jesse had called the bus company and we had a new driver on the way immediately. No shit this really happened.

One special driver will forever be stuck in my mind. I can tell how well a bus tour will go only by a single phone call to Jesse Dupree. During that phone call I ask about the driver. If it is a good driver Jesse will say, *"The driver seems pretty cool."* If the driver is a total fucking dickhead Jesse will say, *"I found a bus but I don't know about the driver, I'll keep looking."* For this particular driver Jesse called me and said, *"I've got us a driver. You'll love this, he reminds me of your dad."* I hung up the phone immediately and thought, *"Oh shit. OH SHIT!"* Jesse was telling the truth. Because my real father's behavior was so similar, from now on in this story I will be calling this bus driver Dad.

When I first met Dad he was sitting in the bus driver's seat.
He was playing southern gospel music so loud that we couldn't
have a conversation. I could tell he wasn't a regular bus driver.
When there was a shortage of bus drivers, truck drivers would fill
in. Trust me when I say that the man who drives chickens
around will drive differently from the man who is used to driving
people around. This man was 68 years old and only had one front
tooth on each side. I could tell Dad was a truck driver because of
his uniform. Cowboy hat (check), western shirt (check), black
leather vest (check) with the standard American Flag pin and
optional NRA pin, pressed blue jeans (check), and vinyl cowboy
boots (check). I walked over to him and tried to greet him over
his holy music. Dad sighed then turned down his music enough
to talk. I told him my name but it was no use. Shouting over his
still pretty loud gospel Dad said, *"Do you have any Indian in you?"*
I yelled back, *"I'm part Cherokee." "You look like an Indian. I'm
going to call you Indian."* It didn't bother me in the slightest
because I have a thicker skin than most these days. I swear to you,
almost every statement this man made was offensive in some way.
We grew to love this gnarly old man and kept him like a racist pet
for the next few months. I could tell Dad drove all over the
country and had no problems getting us from big city to big city.
For the first two weeks he had a lot of trouble getting us to the
gig addresses. I watched him and figured out he could not read.
Sure he knew city names but the man could not read the
sentences on Google Maps. That was in 2005. I didn't make a
big deal out of it and I made sure our road manager was
personally directing us to the gig every damn day.

On to the real story. I had a few questionable run-ins with
Dad. I don't want to go into details but on nights he wasn't
driving he would get really drunk and tell me stories. Some
stories were of him killing gang members who tried to rob the
bus. Some stories were of him running over bums in the tour
bus. I thought the stories were bullshit but he did pull a gun on

me once. It wasn't loaded but how the hell was I supposed to know? But it was all in good fun and remember I'm a southern boy. That wasn't the first time someone had pulled a gun on me. None of that compares to what I am going to tell you next about Dad.

After playing in Green Bay, WI we had some pretty rough partiers come onto the bus. As the crew loaded our gear someone had poured out a decent sized pile of blow on a table in the back of the bus. There were a few lines put out next to the large pile. Dad busted into the back room and asked in his South Georgia accent, *"What the hell are you doin' in here?"* I asked him jokingly, *"Do you want some?"* Dad was a little drunk and he said, *"Want some? I'll show you candy ass motherfuckers how to do it!"* Dad grabbed a straw and instead of snorting one line, he snorted the entire large pile of cocaine right in front of my eyes. Everyone in the room gasped. Dad rose from that table with the face of Mr. Hyde. Without a word, he left the room. We all looked at each other in amazement. I looked at the owner of the blow and he laughed and said, *"Don't worry we have more."* After a few moments my brother came into the room and asked, *"What the hell did you do to the bus driver?! He's out front and it looks like he's dying of a damn heart attack!"* It was winter time in Green Bay and there was 3 feet of snow on the ground. Dad was laid up in the snow having mild convulsions. Roman and I were laughing our ass off but my brother was very concerned. Chris said, *"You guys need to quit laughing. This guy could drop dead any second. What are we going to tell to the cops?"* As soon as he said that Dad ran back onto the bus, straight into the bathroom. One thing about a tour bus you should know is that the toilet is strictly for liquids. That amount of cocaine was total hell on that old man's bowels. Everyone on the bus could hear Dad abusing the toilet. Jesse was banging on the door yelling, *"Goddamn! We'll be hauling your shit for miles!"* Eventually Jesse gave up and the man continued with his emergency intestinal evacuation.

The excitement calmed down and I went to the back of the bus to sleep. A few hours later I heard the bus start up. We were pulling out of Green Bay. I was very curious at this point. There were many scenarios that could have gone down. 1) Dad had died and Jesse had a new bus driver via express delivery. 2) Dad was still alive but the brain-damaged old man was driving the bus and probably about to crash. 3) Dad had survived and pulled through the night. I walked up to the driver's seat out of curiosity. From a distance I could see Dad at the helm. He didn't look right. His hair was completely messed up and he was hunched over. When I got up close enough, I put my hand on his shoulder. As soon as I touched him he shot up, startled and yelled, *"God damn Indian! Are you trying to kill me?!"* When he turned to yell at me I saw his face. He had snorted the cocaine with his right nostril. His right eye was swollen twice its normal size and was a deep red. On top of that, the right side of his face looked numb. Once he stopped yelling he looked back at the road and muttered, *"Y'all mother fuckers can keep your blow. I'm sticking with crank."* The man knew what he liked and I can't argue with that.

    **Mona Lisa – A masterpiece of photography that was taken by Roman Glick. This image was so shockingly bizarre it had to be destroyed upon creation. This was best for all involved.

<> <> <>

Airplanes

    Other than the wear and tear of flying commercially over the years, flying commercial is pretty crappy. The best way to fly is to charter your own plane. It is super convenient but it has its draw backs. Most of the chartered planes are loud and small but you get a good view. These chartered pilots are usually super young and not that experienced. My first chartered flight was in Dodge City, KS, to the twin cities, Minneapolis-St. Paul. We were sitting out near this little old plane when we saw the pilot coming. The pilot was about 80 years old and was pulling a cooler with snacks and sodas (our in-flight meal) and a 12 pack of Budweiser. I was thinking, *"What the hell did I get myself into?"* I always have a sneaking suspicion that all pilots are drunk. But it turned out to be a really cool flight and we got there safely.

The next private charter was really sweet. A multimillionaire mortgager had seen us play in Kansas City and he hired us to play for his 4th of July party at his mansion on the lake of the Ozarks in Kansas. He said he would have his private plane fly us back home. Not only that, he had his plane go ahead of time and pick up all of our wives/girlfriends in Atlanta and bring them back to the party. That was really fucking sweet! After that lavish treatment we never heard from the guy again. We had heard the rumor that he made all of that money with the housing bubble and he lost it all. Hell I don't care how he made the money, they treated us great and we had a blast.

Another private charter was kind of scary. We had to fly from Erie, PA to Oshkosh, WI for the Rock USA Festival. The pilot was from Oshkosh, which is the home to one of the largest air shows in the country. He was there to fly us in a Beechcraft. Our route took us over two great lakes in this little plane. With most chartered flights, the pilots wore at least the professional flying shirt. This guy was dressed just like a cowboy. After he landed to pick us up he got out and said, *"I've got to make a phone call, the right engine is acting up and I'm not sure about it."* Why the fuck would he say something like that? But once again, I bit my tongue and got on the plane. He got us there safe and sound. If you're a pilot don't ever say that shit when you're about to fly over two great lakes. I think that flight was the only time I kissed the damn ground when I got off the plane.

<> <> <>

Vietnam Flash Back

At the time of this story our first album was killing it so we could afford a bunch of cool stuff. We were to play at a festival in Tampa Florida called The Livestock Festival. It's a huge show and hilariously by fate we were opening up for Lynyrd Skynyrd. The highway was backed up for miles and our tour bus was in the middle of it. Our bus driver said he could pull over and talk to the cops about a police escort but we said hell no. I have no idea how it came up but we got the idea of getting a helicopter. Just how our luck happens, just two miles off the highway was a small motel that was empty. We looked up helicopter charter companies and made a few calls. Now this was 4:00 or 5:00 in the evening on a Saturday, so we had no idea what we were going to get. Finally some old guy picked up the phone and yelled, "*HELLLOOO?*" We tell this guy what we needed and where we were. He says back, "*Boys I'm about to go take my wife to dinner but I have about an hour. It takes that long for her to get ready. I know where you're at. It will be $600 and I'll be there in about 20 minutes.*" We send the bus and crew on while we, the band members, wait in the parking lot. About an hour goes by and we were getting nervous. Jesse calls him back asking where the hell he's at. The guy says, "*Turn around.*" There he was, coming across the field next to this shitty motel, was a brand new Aerospatiale helicopter practically having the nose to the ground. Then he whips the helo around and lands right in front of us. He then put the chopper in some sort of idle mode and opens the door. As he approaches he has his hand out for payment. He yelled over the rotors, "*Who's in charge here?*" Jesse says, "*I guess me.*" The pilot yelled back, "*600 big ones chief.*" After Jesse handed him the stack of cash he yells again, "*Hop on in.*" At this point, Jesse leaned over to me and said, "*I think this motherfucker is drunk.*" We got in and it was the nicest helicopter I had ever seen. The interior was just like a limousine. All of the seats were plush leather with very nice carpet. The pilot yells over the radio, "*You boy's want a high-ball?*" I had no idea what he meant. He yelled to me, "*Make me an Old Fashion while you're at it.*" Now an Old Fashion is basically bourbon and cherries. Under our seats, instead of flotation devices there were pull-out coolers with all types of mixers, ice, and all different types of liquor. I just think to myself, *"What the hell?"* We all mix drinks and I handed the pilot his Old Fashion. At that moment, we rocketed into the air. I swear to God that we shot straight up then the nose of the chopper pointed down, going somewhere close to light speed. I started to ask the guy questions to see if he could actually fly or not. I asked, *"So how long have you been flying?"* He yells back, *"I've been flying since I was 17. I flew 8 years in Viet-Fucking-Nam!"* For some reason, with that statement, I was comfortable with this drunk old man flying us to hell. He then did a maneuver that was extremely weird to me. If you have never hovered still in the air, it is like nothing else. At that time, the pilot was comfortable enough to start calling us all chief. He then started talking a lot about Vietnam. I leaned over to my brother Chris and over my head set said, *"I think he thinks we're his old crew from Vietnam."* So instead of backing off with the Vietnam stuff, I had to instigate him. I asked the drunk old pilot, *"So where did the gunner sit?"* He responded with, *"Right behind me, right where you're sitting chief. You want to see how we did it? I've got a few minutes, might was well get your money's worth!"* From that position he tells me to put my head on the glass next to me, looking down at the ground. I do and he said, *"Hang on! This is how we did it!"* He slapped the stick and we started to do a downward spiral. Apparently they would just let the guns blaze in a downward spiral, filling the jungle with lead. Scary shit but I was having the time of my life. Again for some reason, I did not fear for my life.

After that stunt we had to get to the festival. So we take off from getting our money's worth and blazed towards the show. He asked us right before we got there if there was somewhere to land. We told him to put it down right next to the stage. As we circled the stage there was 30,000 people that set their attention away from the opening band to spot this helicopter. We asked the guy if we could drop Jackyl Dollars out into crowd. These

Jackyl Dollars were basically $5 off coupons you could use at a record store for our new album. The pilot said, "*Hell fuckin yeah! We use to drop leaflets out on villages in Vietnam all the time!*" So we dropped stacks of these coupons out of the side of the chopper and the wind pushed most of them into an adjacent pond. The crowd thought it was real money so we saw hundreds of people jumping into this pond. It was hilarious! But we had to land. At this point, the pilot was acting like a *Jackyl*.

We saw the clearing near the stage and instead of doing a nice soft landing, he slung us around and did a combat dive. We didn't really anticipate the amount of wind this chopper would make. It was like a lawnmower the size of Wal-Mart blowing grass, dust, and then tents all over! If you remember that we kicked off the Lynyrd Skynyrd tour because we ruined their dinner one night. Well in this helicopter ride we knocked over their entire dinning tent. Even to this day I almost piss myself laughing at the irony. This old, salty, ex Vietnam pilot knew exactly what was up and really boosted this event into a publicity stunt from hell! Where he put us down 30,000 people could see who was getting out of this chopper. The last thing this pilot told us was, "*Alright boys, you go kick their fucking asses!*" To salute this veteran, we did just that. We got out of the chopper and ran to our tour bus. I sat down, got a big drink, and could not believe I got out of that alive!

<> <> <>

Rent Me, Roll Me, Carry Me Off!

Over the years we have rented a lot of vehicles. Let me tell you, we always got the premium insurance. It does not matter who is driving in *Jackyl* that damn rental car gets beat to hell. Here is where I let you find out who does most of the damage.

<> <> <>

Machine Gun Fire

Before we recorded our first record in LA we did a demo at a friend's studio in Memphis that was right on the Mississippi

River. We had a rental van for us to get around in and move our gear. From where the studio was, there was an adjacent office building with a parking lot out front. Next to the office building there was a Spaghetti Warehouse restaurant. Connecting the studio to Spaghetti Warehouse was about a half mile of gravel road. It was convenient because we didn't have to use the highway. Jesse Dupree was of course driving and we all go over to Spaghetti Warehouse to eat. Instead of driving like a normal sane person, this fool floored it and drove all the way there in reverse. He then backed the van all the way up to the front door of the building so close we had to climb out of the back. Because we were also using the van to haul gear around, there were no seats. We were all rolling around in the back on the floor when Jesse was doing this bullshit. It was a pretty violent ride! After we finished eating we had to do the same window bullshit to get in. Jesse had to one up the way he came there so instead of backing up, he floors it into a sideways drift the entire length of the gravel road. All of us were slung around and we screamed our heads off for Jesse to quit.

We finally make it back and Jesse and Chris go into the studio. Being slung around, we needed a joint to calm our nerves. Tom Bettini (Ex-Jackyl) picked himself up off the floor and got into the driver's seat. We fired up a joint and tried to relax after that hell ride when suddenly a furious woman started to bang on the window. She was screaming, "*Do you know what you did?! Do you know?*" Tom yelled back, "*I DIDN'T DO SHIT!*" She then yelled again, "*I SAW YOU DRIVING!*" Tom then started to get upset, "*NO YOU DIDN'T YA BITCH!*" We all got out to see what the hell the problem was. Apparently, when Jesse had drifted the van sideways he had thrown gravel at all of the cars in that business parking lot. He had knocked out literally 20 windshields. Some of those cars were so bad it looked like there was severe hail damage. I went into the studio to get Jesse. We had to get the insurance information of all of those people. I couldn't bear to look but my brother Chris came back inside of the studio and said, "*You ain't gonna believe it! There's 2 or 3 inches of gravel on some of those hoods!*" This rental van was not destroyed but instead used as a tool of mass destruction!

<> <> <>

The Dodge K Car, The "K" is for Krap!

This story starts the day we were going out to LA to record our first record. When we landed, Geffen Records had two rental cars waiting for us to use for the few months we would be in LA recording. We got off the plane all pretty drunk but we were extremely fired up about our first record. We went to the Hertz rental desk and they handed us the keys. Then the rental agents followed us out to the parking lot to show us where our cars were. We were expecting some sort of bad ass car because Geffen Records has a ton of money. The rental car lady dumped us off in front of two Dodge K Cars. If you do not know what they are, they are the worst cars Dodge ever built. It's a 4 door, front wheel drive, piece of shit. In one car Jesse would be driving with Tom, and Chris. In my car was me, Jesse's brother Danny (driving), and Jimmy Stiff. At the last little booth they gave us our receipts. Once Jesse had that slip in his hand, that lunatic was gone. We were sitting behind him not knowing what to do. Little three inch high concrete dividers were laid out in a snake fashion leading to the highway. Jesse, with his foot to the floor, went straight over all of the barriers. All of the rental people just stared at their K Car going full rally car. Sparks were flying. We had to drive as fast as we could just to keep up because Jesse was the only one with the directions. As soon as Jesse made it to the freeway he whipped the shit out of the car and swerved into traffic. I had no idea how the hell he didn't get hit or hit someone else. Once we were both on the freeway, my car had to swerve around other cars just to keep Jesse in sight. The sign for where we were staying, Canoga Park, came into view but Jesse blasted past it. As we approached the next light, it turned from yellow to red. My car gradually slowed down but Jesse kept barreling towards the intersection. We thought he was trying to kill himself but at the very possible last second, he slams on the brakes. All four tires locked up and an extremely loud screech was heard in a 5 block radius. In his defense, he did stop for the light.

We pulled up next to him at a light and asked where the hell he was going. Jesse rolls his window down and said, "*Let's go down Hollywood Boulevard. We're in Los Angles to do our first record; we have to go down Hollywood Boulevard!*" So we went for it. In front of the old Tower Records store, Jesse decided to take a violent U-turn into traffic... again. When that son of a bitch came about, he hit the curb and a hubcap flew off. That hubcap rolled onto the sidewalk and hit a guy in the leg! Jesse saw what happened and gunned it. I thought we were going to jail before we recorded a single note.

We headed towards our apartments. When we finally got there, we parked our car on the street in front of the apartments. As I got out of the car, Jesse missed my door by inches and got out of sight. We could hear the whine of a car the next block over. It was not the sound of a muscle car, it was a breezy strain. Just like when someone draws their last breath. Jesse was on a one-way street but that mula-fucka came back the same way going balls to the wall. Danny, Jimmy Stiff, and I were out of the car watching this spectacle. Jesse was heading right for us and had floored it like he was drag racing. He hit the curb and the car launched into the air about two feet. Pretty impressive if you ask me. The car landed less than a foot from ours and hit the curb with a violent crunch/thud. After that sound, I swear to God, the car let out a human moan. Then, the car was dead, very dead. This son of a bitch didn't even have electric power. It was like Jesse had severed the car's spinal cord. Less than an hour after we picked up the car, we called the rental company and told them to send someone to get the piece of shit that died on us "unexpectedly". An old black guy came with a tow truck and he asked us what happened. Jesse said to the guy, in an innocent fashion, "*It just died.*" The tow truck guy inspected the car further. There was no visible exterior damage but he noticed the outsides of the tires were completely worn. He looked at all of us and said, "*WHAT IN THE HELL HAPPENED TO THESE TIRES?*" Innocently we said, "*It was like that when we picked it up.*"

<><><>

Keeping Up with the Jackyls

As time went on, the fascinating stories of our rental car destruction had been circulating around many bands in the industry. Eventually it got back to our record company, Geffen Records. These stories had turned into legends, like I said, other bands were coming up to us to ask about it. We were playing at a club in Nashville called the Cannery. Our good friend, a guy who really helped us in getting signed, Todd Sullivan (from Geffen) came out from LA to hang with us and watch our show. He had heard of our rental car escapades and wanted to keep up with us. When he arrived (in a rental car of course), he asked where Jesse Dupree was. You couldn't have timed it any better. Jesse pulled up in a rental car from the airport. The parking lot of this club was dirt and Jesse took the opportunity to start doing donuts. We eventually had to dive out of the way. Todd asked, "*Who the hell is this guy?*" I yelled, "*Who? That motherfucker is Jesse! You should have known!*"

Later that night we had an awesome show so we were going back to the hotel to party. Now Todd wasn't necessarily drunk but he had enough drinks in him to give him the courage to try to best our rental stories. As we were heading back from the show, Todd was driving with my brother Chris. Leaving the parking lot, Todd floors it right off of a 5 foot embankment. The drop was so steep that the hood just slammed on the ground and we could only see the taillights in the air. That shit was hilarious.

Todd earned our rental respect. After then he was JFL (Jackyl for Life). The car though, not so much.

CHAPTER FIVE

THINGS YOU SEE IN A GYM

Having a career in rock, I've had to keep in shape. With all of the shitty food and lifestyle on the road, it is hard to be good. So every day I hit the gym. This collection of stories is about all of the crazy places I've been while working out on the road. There are few categories of "gyms" in my world. You have health clubs, fitness centers, and meat-head establishments. Health clubs are really spas that have a focus on working out. Fitness centers are a good middle of the road gym. And the meat-head establishments have only one focus; pumping iron. Here are a few highlights of what it takes to stay in shape on the road.

< > < > < >

The Philadelphia Experience

While on tour with Aerosmith once, we rolled through Philly. When we get to our venue we called a taxi to come take us to a gym. When we get into the taxi we were told the gym was only 5 miles away. During our ride the meter kept racking up. 40 minutes later we arrive at this ratty looking gym. We got out and got slammed with an $80 cab fare. Me and my gym buddies pooled our money together just to pay this ridiculous sum. As I was getting my gym bag out of the taxi trunk I looked over to see the damn tour bus just off in the distance. One of my band members flips out and said we weren't paying shit. The taxi driver freaked out and called the cops. Eventually we all settled on just $60. To the cab drivers defense the only way to get from the tour bus to the gym, was the extremely long route or walk a couple hundred yards through a swamp. That day God was picking on me.

<> <> <>
The Brother went SNAP!

This next story makes me laugh to this day. The set up at this specific gym had the work stations on the ground floor and cardio equipment on the second floor. This layout gave me the perfect vantage point of the gym while running on the treadmill. On this day I had finished my workout and it was time for my cardio. In came this insanely ripped black guy, wearing a bright stripped leotard, who looked like a cross between Mr. T and the Ultimate Warrior. Now this guy walked up to the squatting machine and had to make it known to everyone in that gym that he was squatting all of the weight available. He made a complete production of setting all of the weights up. I watched intently. With a loud shout, this muscular black guy shouldered the bar and began to squat. At the bottom of his squat, there was a sound of something that sounded like a wet 2x4 being split in half. He let out a like scream of horror. He had literally ripped his scrotum! I was immediately disgusted. After a few seconds, I started to giggle. I had to go to the locker room because I started to laugh so hard. I felt bad. The paramedics were called in. Just as a note: They had a neck brace for when you break your neck in an accident. Well when you rip your nut sack, the paramedics have a device that keeps your legs spread. I call it the "Taint Restraint!" To describe it, if a billiards rack had sex with a neck brace then their child would be The Taint Restraint. This only added to the comedy. All I could think of was what my grandmother would say to me and my brother, "*That's what you get for showin' out! Hurt and embarrassed!*"

<> <> <>
The German Gym

While we were on tour in Europe, we went over to Munster, Germany to open for ZZ top at a huge outdoor festival. We were staying in the town of Munster but the actual venue was around 20 miles outside of town. I have to take a second and describe

Munster to you. Munster is the most picturesque German village you could ask for. The scenery is beautiful, the people are extremely nice, and the hotel was amazing. The only problem I had with my stay was that the beds seemed to be made for children. Other than that, here's what I remember of Munster.

We arrived on a Friday and we did not have to play until Saturday night. Something about the beautiful scenery changed something inside of many *Jackyl* members. Instead of wanting to get ripped in the gym, most of the band wanted to ride bikes around like Mary Poppins. It had been a couple of days since I had worked out and bike riding wasn't going to cut it. So off I went with my guitar tech to the hotel's exercise room. I must emphasize once again that the hotel was very nice but once I walked into the gym, it seemed like I was back in the Middle Ages. I can only describe this German gym as "homemade". ("Homemade" by my local Gold's Gym standards)

I completed my makeshift work out that was really 50 variants of a single chest exercise. After that, I had the need to sweat out the nights of partying so my buddy and I went to the sauna. One thing I love about European saunas is that you can crank those sons of bitches as high as you want. If you want to literally cook yourself, you can. After our workout my buddy and I got into this horseshoe-shaped sauna and sat down. My buddy was propped up in the far corner and I was sitting directly in front of the glass door. I had a perfect view of the entire gym. After a few moments of sweating, an elderly German couple came into my view in front of the glass door. They looked around the gym slightly confused then slowly shuffled to some chairs near the door in front of me. Then the German couple started to strip. I thought the old woman was going to come in with only her panties and bra. Oh no, she whipped her bra off to expose the largest breasts I have ever seen. I was in shock and thinking, "*Oh hell no, she isn't coming in here like that is she*"? I looked over at my buddy and was going to warn him but I stopped myself. His headphones were on and his eyes were closed so I decided to wait. This woman dropped her underwear to show a gigantic hairy bush. This bush started under her armpits and then swooped down to her knees. This mass of pubic hair was probably a half foot deep and it looked like a baseball catcher's protective armor. I looked over to what I think is her husband and I'm staring at three inches of uncircumcised penis. From my in field research, my professional opinion is that almost all European men are uncircumcised and smoke at least 3 packs of unfiltered cigarettes a day. The couple came into the sauna and my buddy popped his head up and took them all in one sight. Instead of being shocked, he started giggling like a little girl. When they sat down I had enough so I left as soon as possible. With all of the elderly nudity I could not tell if I was there for a second or hours.

We returned to our rooms with tales of hairy Munsters but we found out that the rest of the band had been taken out to eat with our Geffen Records representative. So we decided to get something to eat at the hotel restaurant. I just wanted something light to eat before we headed out to the venue. I had no idea that dinner was going to take three hours. It took us an hour just to finish the first of six courses. When the check finally came, we realized that we had to split a $300 bill. My friend, who at this point in the 90's looked just like Joe Dirt, said *"Hey man, I haven't gotten paid for next week, I'm a little short."* I said, *"You just got paid yesterday! How much do you need?!"* He pulled out his wallet and only produced a $5 American bill. I said, *"Only five fucking dollars?"* Lucky for him, the rest of the guys showed up with the record rep who paid for our dinner and we all piled into a mini-van to go to the venue. As soon as this van gets onto the Autobahn, our driver slammed the pedal to the mother fucking floor. That van must have gotten up to 110 mph and the driver was chain smoking the whole way. About 5 miles out of the venue we started to smell it. Try to imagine 30,000 people that had not showered in days. Hey I can't judge, that's rock for you.

We made it to the venue just in time to see Destiny's Child. I was only in Munster, Germany for 48 hours but my life was impacted forever.

<><><>

The #1 Meat-Head Establishment

The names and locations of this story have been changed (but not really!) to protect the innocents (mostly me). I was somewhere in either Maryland or West Virginia when I was searching for a gym. Our runner/driver said her brother-in-law had a gym and she'd take us there. I didn't ask how far it was, which was my first mistake. After 30 minutes cramped in a car, I was finally leaving the city. Buildings were replaced by corn fields and herds of cows. An hour later we arrived and the first thing I noticed was the sign. It looked like the Gold's Gym logo was copied by a 4th grader. Where the word "Gold's" should have been, Kelly's Gym was written sloppily over the top. The second thing I noticed was that everyone in the gym, including the owner, was standing outside waiting for us. They all greeted us when we got out of the car. I thought it was really nice but it was like The Twilight Zone. When I finally got inside I was amazed. There were no leg presses, no treadmills, and no leg equipment whatsoever. Along the walls were an army of bench presses. I swear to God there must have been at least 10,000 pounds of bench press weight alone. One thing I forgot to tell you was that these guys had some of the most developed upper bodies I had ever seen but their legs were sticks. I am not joking when I say that their arms would not fit in their pants. On that day, leaving Kelly's Gym, I knew then I would never see another literal army of bench presses like that again in my life.

<><><>

The Perils of Staying in Shape

When you travel for a living and work out every day, just getting to and from a gym is a real adventure. I'm sure some of you have heard or maybe even seen steroid use in the gym. It might not be that common to see in plain sight but it is there. I have seen steroids, heavy drinking, and cocaine as someone's pre-workout ritual. When you are working out, the mentality should be improving your health and helping your body, not tearing it down with drugs and alcohol. The drugs might sound crazy but that isn't even the weirdest thing I have seen in a gym. This is my countdown of the top three strangest things Jeff Worley has seen in a gym/health club.

#3 Now what I am going to try to explain here may be shocking. Reader's discretion is advised. I have to spread the word about what I call a 'buoy'. The buoy's home turf is usually in a health club or YMCA where the pool is in sight of the sauna. A buoy is a fat, creepy perverted man who floats around in the pool exposing his eyes and nose out of the water like a hippo. You can't see his hands but you know he's touching *something*. They float closest to the sauna, waiting for their prey. Their prey could be anyone; man, woman or child. But most of the time it is any sweaty guy coming out of the sauna. The innocent prey isn't expecting a masturbating manatee only feet away. There is no defense for a buoy but I think there should be warning signs posted so everyone is aware. Would that be politically correct?

#2 The YMCA is ground zero where I saw my 2nd strangest thing in a gym. I was reading some medical magazine in an article that said after the age of 60, a man's scrotum will stretch 3 inches a year for the next 10 years. So you will have an extra 30 inches of ball-sack by the time you're 70! My brother being the biggest skeptic of my medical knowledge, said I was full of shit, especially about this. The only person we could have tested this on was our father, and he would have frowned upon us for even asking.

In one YMCA, there couldn't have been a better set up to see this phenomenon in person. The sauna of this YMCA was right next to the hot tub and the only thing separating the two was a pane of glass. While sitting in the sauna, I was jamming with my ear phones on when my brother taps me on the shoulder. I looked over to only see his mouth moving. I took my ear buds off to hear him say, *"Jeff, you really weren't shitting me about those old man balls."* He then pointed over to the hot tub. I looked up and froze. There I saw an old man crawling out of the hot tub completely naked. There were stairs and a rail but the old gentleman chose to crawl out of this hot tub. We were then visually assaulted by his asshole and the base of his balls. I swear to god he was three feet out of the tub before his balls were on dry land! At that moment, in that YMCA, my medical knowledge was vindicated. The only thing my brother Chris did was shake his head in defeat. Apparently the only other person that has been spreading this obscure medical knowledge is Johnny Knoxville because of certain scenes in his hit film 'Bad Grandpa'.

#1 Now I think my wife has one of the best asses in the world. Being in a rock band I have seen thousands of amazing women with great asses. Being a straight guy who is comfortable with his sexuality I have no problem telling this story.

I was sitting in a locker room of a gym in Allentown, PA. Earlier there was an old man working out on a stair climber and the only thing that caught my eye was how fucking steep he had the machine set to. If 10 was the setting for straight up, he had that son of a bitch to 11. After my workout, I was in the locker room when the old man walked right up to me. His locker was right beside mine. That's when it happened, his towel fell. His torso was of an old shriveled man, his legs were equally aged. I cannot tell a lie here, but that old man's ass looked like it belonged to an 18 year old blonde girl. It was plump, round, and covered in peach fuzz! I wish I had proof of this but I couldn't just take a picture of a naked guy's ass in the gym. I couldn't go up to the guy and say, *"Hey I'm in town with my band and I'll give you tickets to the show if you show my buddies your perfect ass!"* When I went back to the bus to tell my buddies I might as well have said I saw Big Foot flying a UFO because no one in the world would believe me. How's that for a #1 for you?

CHAPTER SIX

CELEBRITY SIGHTINGS

< > < > < >

Chuck Woolery, The Game Show Host

When I started out traveling for music my grandmother would always ask me the same question when I got home. "Did you see anyone famous?" Well, Grandma, here is your answer. Chuck Woolery. Yes, the game show host. Chuck might not be the most famous guy in my collection but he was the first famous person I met so I had to put him first.

Before we started our first record, we still had to tour up and down the east coast, for nothing. (i.e. no money). We had a gig in New Jersey and a day off. A day off for *Jackyl* usually meant trouble. Being so close to the city, we wanted to go downtown New York City for the evening. At that time, I hadn't been to such a big city before. We all piled into our old dodge van (the orange one) and headed in. After driving down Times Square and taking it all in, we quickly became completely lost and could see the city disappearing behind us. Thankfully we were in a wealthier part of New York City with townhouses and 5 star restaurants. Remember, this was before any portable GPS. We had to stop and actually ask for directions. I saw a man in a tuxedo with two beautiful blonde women on the street and we pulled the van right up to them. Because the passenger door was broken, I opened the side doors. I was afraid he was thinking he was being kidnapped. I yelled out in my southern accent, *"Sir, could you tell us the way back to Times Square?"* The man walked over and without hesitation, pops his head into the van and says, *"Where the hell are you boys from?"* I say, *"Holy shit! Chuck*

Woolery!" Yes it was none other than the original host of Wheel of Fortune and The Love Connection, Chuck Woolery. I told him we were in a rock band called *Jackyl* and were from down south. He was cool as hell! He told us where to stay out of and how to get back to Times Square. He was so cool that we asked him if he would like to hang out of with us. Chuck smiled, gestured towards the two smoking hot blondes, and said, "*Boys, I think I have things covered right here. Good luck.*" I thought, "*Wow!*"

<><><>

Justin Timberlake / Kid Rock

We were in Detroit and were invited to Kid Rock's house for a party. Once we got there, Roman and I headed down to Kid Rock's pool to chill and have a few beers. There were two nice looking older women laying out in the sun by the pool. I had a joint on me but I didn't want to offend those ladies because I wasn't sure who they were and I didn't want to get kicked out for offending what could possibly be Kid Rock's mother. We sat down on some lounge chairs and after a few minutes the ladies came up and introduced themselves. One of women said, "*I'm Justin's mother. Justin will be here soon.*" I thought to myself, "*Who is Justin?*" But we talked a bit, then went inside to eat some BBQ when two black Lincoln Town cars pulled up. The lady then said, "*Oh Justin is here with his girlfriend.*" At that time I realized she was talking about Justin Timberlake. He was dating Cameron Diaz then. Cameron is as beautiful in real life as she is on screen. Anyway, a joint comes out and we start chatting with everyone and getting high. It took no time to find out that Justin is a pretty cool dude. He is originally from rural Tennessee and hasn't forgotten his roots . Once we got comfortable Justin asked me if I wanted to go inside and help him roll a joint. I, of course, said hell yeah! Back inside he whipped out a big bag of weed, I mean it was probably around a half ounce. He tells me to roll it up. I asked, "*All of it?!*" He said, "*All of it!*" So he brought these

long rolling papers out and we rolled up a Cheech and Chong
style massive joint. People gathered around and we fired the son
of a bitch up. I didn't know much about Justin Timberlake but
one thing was bugging me and eventually I had to ask him. I
looked right at him and said, *"I read in the National Enquirer
that a couple of weeks ago you played a live show with Michael
Jackson. It said that Michael's nose fell off and you accidentally
kicked it off the stage while dancing. PLEASE tell me that's the
truth!"* Justin giggled and Cameron was laughing her ass off.
Justin said, *"No, none of that shit is true."* Dammit foiled again by
the National Enquirer! That night we had a show so he headed
off to our venue to rock the fucking house. Before we left they
invited us to their show the next day, but they didn't tell us any
information about it.

That next morning Justin's camp had already gotten in
contact with Jesse and asked what we liked to eat because they
were having some sort of cook out. I thought to myself, "Damn,
these people are nice!" So we go to their show that night and it
was something very different from the rock world. They told us
to come around to the bus entrance and someone would be
waiting for us. When we arrived there were two guys in suits
looking like some rent-a-secret service dude who waved us
through. The cook-out was where the busses were parked but
they had more than one bus. Justin had 5 damn buses for him
and his people! And how they had them parked, they had
blocked off a big square for our cook out. It was like an old west
wagon train. Justin's mom greeted us and gave us our passes.
Then they got the food going and it was very cool. As a side note,
that evening was the first and last time in my life I will ever ride
one of those Segway contraptions! Here's why. During this
cook-out everyone was partying and having a good time. Out of
the corner of my eye I saw two Segways parked by one of the
busses. Justin saw me looking at them and said, *"You guys can do
whatever you want with them."* While maybe slightly under the

influence, I got on top of one and tried to gun it. It flipped right out from underneath me and I crashed it. Justin didn't seem too upset about it.

Performing at the show that night was The Black Eyed Peas, Christina Aguilera, with Justin Timberlake headlining. I asked Justin's mom where I could go with the pass I had. She said I could go anywhere with it so I said, "*Cool I'm going to watch Christina Aguilera.*" She turned and looked right at me, "*No you're not. If you are going to use that guest pass to watch her you better just leave.*" I was shocked. She totally turned on me. It was like a female version of Dr. Jekyll and Mr. Hyde, I'm still scared to even look at Christina to this day. I have yet to see Christina play live. So I didn't go watch her but I really didn't give a damn in the first place. I knew who invited me and I was respectful to them. Apparently there was some drama between the Justin camp and the Christina camp because of some sort of competitive bullshit.

After the cookout it was time for Justin's show. I have been to all types of concerts but the only exception was a pop concert. It's really not my thing at all. The one MAJOR difference is that out of 20,000 people, there were probably 19,450 women there. The rest of the crowd was split between Dads that were slowly dying inside and gay men having the time of their lives. When the lights went down, the screaming started. The normal sound of a crowd tells me it is time to rock but the screeching of that many girls was honestly horrifying. In Justin's defense that shows was fucking awesome. After the show we hung out on Justin's main bus. I have to say that bus was kick ass. There was even a damn tanning bed in it! Once again I was impressed. Justin and his people are some of the nicest I have ever met. I would hang with them at any time. To wrap things up I could have taken a picture of us smoking dope and sold it to The National Inquirer for a lot of money. In this day and age of legalization, everyone knows everyone gets high. I didn't write this story to cash in; I just wanted people to know I got high with Justin Timberlake, Cameron Diaz, and Justin's mom. It was awesome!

Then there was Kid Rock. The first time we met Bobby was at The Machine Shop in Flint, Michigan. To me, it is one of the greatest rock venues left in the country and owned by our good friend Kevin Zink. One night, Kid Rock actually came up on stage with a chainsaw and did The Lumberjack with Jesse. Because of that, we were invited to his house the next time we were in town. That's what led up to the story above. That Christmas we were also invited to Kid Rock's personal Christmas party. When we showed up we realized it wasn't a bunch of random people. It was just his family, his band, and some famous hockey players. He had taped his Christmas special and we watched it while getting drunk. Once we were all drunk, Kid Rock said, *"Let's all go to the barn and jam."* On our way to the barn we saw some sort of lighted bowling pins that were lining his drive way. At that time Roman Glick had been juggling a lot and was getting pretty damn good at it. I asked Bobby to juggle his Christmas bowling pin. I turned to him and said, "I bet Roman can juggle those bowling pin Christmas ornaments." Of course we immediately broke them. He said not to worry about it but after that Christmas party we never heard from him again. So here is a personal note to Kid Rock: If you are mad at us for the juggling incident, I'm sorry. Let me know what the cost is and I'll buy you a new one. In our defense you did get us drunk as hell and we all had a great time.

<> <> <>

Tex Cobb

If you don't know of or have ever seen Randal "Tex" Cobb, he's an actor and ex-boxer that has been in films such as Raising Arizona, Ace Ventura: Pet Detective, and Ernest Goes to Jail. After his professional boxing career he was cast in a lot of movies as a big fucking scary guy.

Once our first record went gold, our lawyer Jim Zumwalt invited us to his office for a Christmas party in Nashville. I think he felt obligated to invite us because we were selling more records than anyone in the room. The party was filled with country singers/song writers and we were the turd in the punch bowl. It was nice that they invited us to the ass kissing party but it wasn't our cup of tea. After shaking everyone's hands we stood in the corner and tried to be good and not embarrass ourselves for 'Zummy's' sake. After 20 minutes of just talking to ourselves I noticed a big dude coming into the room. Let me tell you, he was gnarlier than shit. He looked like he was about to kill someone. He started to scan the room with his crazy eyes. We were all watching him and then he suddenly locked on to us. I turned my head away immediately. He watched us for a little bit then a dainty little woman came up and kissed him. Chris, my brother turned to me and said, *"Jeff you know who that is? He's been in movies."* I said, *"Yeah, that's fuckin' Tex Cobb!"* Tex and the lady chatted a little bit and we could hear his grunts across the room. She kissed him again and walked away. Tex walked over to a table with food on it. He picked up a cookie, took a bite, and then grunted as he threw the cookie back on the pile. Then he locked on to us and started to walk towards us. I whispered to everyone, *"Dear God, here comes Tex Cobb."* He came right up to us and yelled, *"Who the hell are you? Y'all don't look like you're supposed to be here."* We told him we were in the band *Jackyl.* He shouted back in my face, *"I've heard of you, you're alright for white boys."* (To this day I still don't know what that means.) He then asked what we were drinking and we held up a bottle of whiskey. We then take a shot together and start chatting. My translation of the conversation from Tex was *"This party sucks and the people here are lame."* I say that in my best language. He said his wife was a country song writer and that's the only reason he was there. We laughed and agreed because that was the only option when talking with Tex Cobb. But I have got to tell you, Tex was cooler than shit. He then said, *"Boys I'm out!"* We took another shot of whiskey and he was gone. He didn't say goodbye to anyone. This lasted all of five minutes from the time he walked in the door.

<> <> <>

Evel 'EVIL' Knievel

We ironically met one of my childhood heroes, Evel Knievel, on our Guinness Book World Record 100 Shows in 50 Days tour. We were in Tampa, Florida doing a radio show hosted by Bubba the Love Sponge. If you've never heard of Bubba, he's a syndicated radio host that makes Howard Stern look like Mother Teresa. The story goes; Bubba was fired from one radio job because he had a hog slaughtered on air. That's rock n' roll baby! To make the tour work and to meet Guinness standards, we had to play two shows a day. Both shows had to be a minimum of 20 minutes so we would play 30 minutes in the morning and a full show at night. In the morning we would usually play in a Wal-Mart parking lot somewhere with the local radio station hosting it. At night was the big venue and a full show. The morning show would be at 6:30 so kids could come before school and adults could come before work. After we played we would sign autographs for the fans twice a day. This was a very large crowd for an autograph session, around 2000 people. One night after signing autographs for about an hour I noticed a guy on a big Harley street bike weaving through the crowd, blowing past all of the security, and was coming straight for us. As he got within a few feet of the signing table, my smart ass said really loudly, *"Who does this mother fucker think he is, Evel Knievel?"* He cut his motorcycle off and coasted right up to our table. The man got up, took off his helmet, extended his hand and said, *"Hey Jackyl boys, I'm Evel Knievel."* I was in shock. This is when I knew God was picking on me. I shook the daredevil's hand. Let me explain some humor and irony to you. Because of our song Lumberjack, I had shaken hands with lumberjacks that have had severe hand injuries due to bad accidents on the job. Evel's hands told the story of his life. They were completely messed up because of all of his failed stunts. There was no doubt he had broken every bone in his body over time. He died some years after that so I'm glad I met him. I have the picture to prove it.

<> <> <>

Sweet, Sweet, Connie

Yes, the same Connie mentioned in the iconic Grand Funk Railroad song 'We're an American Band'. The Lyrics go, *"Sweet, sweet, Connie, she's doing her act, she had the whole show and that's a natural fact."* We would go on to do a cover of that song and have her in our music video. We met her long before that though. Connie Hamzy is the most famous groupie in the world who has allegedly performed oral sex on hundreds of well known people from Huey Lewis to rumored Bill Clinton. It's hard to remember exactly when I met her but I believe it was on an Aerosmith tour. Someone said that Sweet Connie was coming to the gig. An Aerosmith roadie said she was going to blow everybody. I asked, *"You mean that Connie from the Funk song?"* He said, *"Who else would it be?"* The band members in Aerosmith didn't really want her around but the crew was a different story. I think there were at least 72 guys on that tour and Connie literally blew all of them. She was busy all day. I've never seen anything like it before. Her services did not come free. She wanted shirts, front row tickets, back stage passes, beer, and a catering ticket. In that way she was a very smart business woman. She even came out with a book that told in detail all of her exploits.

Fast forward to 1997. We did our *'We're an American Band'* music video that featured Connie. Jesse had warned her not to mention blowing anyone or anything sexual because our wives and children were at the video shoot. To her defense she behaved herself all day and at the end Jesse thanked everyone who worked on the video. He personally thanked Connie for being there.

She responded with an innocent look on her face with all of our wives and children that were within ear shot, *"See Jesse I told you I wouldn't try to suck anyone's cock!"* Everyone paused and stared at her. The only thing I could do was laugh my ass off. This leads us to our next story. (If you can find Connie's book, get it!)

<> <> <>

Huey Lewis

As fate would have it, I had just read Sweet Connie's book of her sexual exploits during a flight over seas. We were on tour with Aerosmith in Europe when we played in Milan, Italy. Playing at this show was us, actual Tibetan monks, Zakk Wylde's 'Pride and Glory', the thrash band Sepultura, White Snake, (I'm not making this shit up) and Huey Lewis. European shows start really early so the monks went on at 9:00 AM, then we played, then Pride and Glory. Zakk Wylde came into our dressing room around 9:15 with a large bottle of Jack Daniels (the one with the handle). We all got extremely drunk before the Monks played. As the Monks went on stage I realized this was not a band called The Tibetan Monks, these were real authentic monks. The rumor was that a kid from Harvard flew over to Tibet and recorded these monks doing their thing on a cassette tape. He took that recording back to America and made a record. That record sold 10 million copies and The Monks went on tour. Let me tell you, when you're drunk at 9:30 in the morning watching Monks play for Italian metal fans, you can only laugh your ass off! We had a pretty good set and when we came off the stage, there stood none other than Huey Lewis, coming out of his tour bus.

Back to Connie's book. This specific piece of literature names Huey's penis as the biggest in the music business. It was pretty funny that right after learning the truth, Huey Lewis was right there! Huey approached us and said, *"John Kalodner told me you boys were over here. You know he's a friend of mine."* So he already had the run down on us. Right after that I had to ask him, *"Hey*

I've got to ask you something. We just finished Connie Hamzy's book. Is it true that you have the biggest dick in the business?" Huey just hung his head and grinned. He then said, *"That book came out a week before I asked my fiancé to marry me. I'm just glad that I'm on the top of the scale. I'd hate to be Peter Frampton."* According to Connie, she named Peter Frampton as having the smallest penis she had ever mouthed.

To keep up the insanity of this story, when we returned from Europe, we played our first North American show in Toronto. We got there a day early and the promoter invited us out to see the venue. We had no idea what the lineup was or what has happening. We were just glad to be on the ground for a minute. When we got to the show that night, guess who was playing? Peter Frampton himself. He is a legend, a guitar god, and he had an amazing show that night. But the only thing I could think about was his little penis, which I will now call "Little Pete". Tell me, can I really make this shit up?!

<><><>

Adam Sandler

This story is short but it's a meeting with a major movie star. It must have been 1994 or 1995 and we were on tour opening for Aerosmith. We were staying at my favorite hotel in Los Angeles, The Mondrian. You could see all types of famous people there. You could go up the elevator with a rock star and come down with a movie star. This hotel can accommodate you in almost every way 24 hours a day, 7 days a week.

After eating a huge meal one night, I needed to hit the gym. It was about 3:00 a.m. I had been in that exact gym at the same hour before and I was surprised that there was a guy already in there. Because of the limited weights, you really had to share the equipment. Out of nowhere, this guy asks me over to spot him while he was bench pressing. I didn't know his name but I recognized him as a guy from Saturday Night Live. I actually said, *"Hey aren't you on Saturday Night Live?"* He introduced himself as Adam Sandler. I asked what he was doing in LA. He said, *"I'm here doing my first film 'Air Heads."* He asked who I was here with and I told him, *"I'm with my band Jackyl."* He said, *"I love your song with the chainsaw!"* From the beginning I could tell he was going to be something big just the way he carried himself and how cool he was.

<> <> <>

Sam Kinison

Right after we signed our first record deal, Geffen Records flew us out to LA to get a real taste for the city. The first time we were in Los Angles we were poor, this time we were given $500 a week just for food. We were staying at the Hyatt Hotel on Sunset Blvd. That hotel was known as the 'Riot House' because of all of the hardcore partying. This was where the legend of Led Zeppelin's partying happened. We were sitting at the hotel patio bar having a few drinks and watching the cars on Sunset Blvd. This was on April 8Th, 1992. All of a sudden the patio door opens and the great comedian Sam Kinison steps out. He looked around and yells, *"Hey!"* at us in his classic tone. In my southern accent I yell back, *"Holy shit it's Sam Kinison!"* If I had a damn camera with us back then, you would be looking at a picture of us with that big funny guy. After hearing my southern accent he asked (just like most of these celebrities) *"Where the hell are you boys from?"* We explained we were from the south and were in a band called *Jackyl.* We wanted to buy him a drink but he turned it down because he was "on the wagon". I guess that meant he was sober. After a quick chat he wished us the best of luck. He then disappeared through the same door he came out of. Unfortunately we learned a week later, while in our rehearsal studio, that Sam Kinison was killed in a car wreck just days after we met him. I wish I had made this shit up.

<> <> <>

David Lee Roth

My first and only meeting with the great David Lee Roth was in Greenville, SC. A friend of ours, Sam Tingle, who worked for Universal Records, gave me and Jesse Dupree tickets and back stage passes to David Lee Roth's show. This was the early 90's and he was on one of his solo tours and was not playing with Steve Vai. After the show we were invited back to a small party for David Lee's guests. We were ushered into a dark room that had a disco ball in the middle of the fucking ceiling. Once we were there, David's road manger came into the room grabbed a karaoke microphone and boomed in an introduction voice, *"Ladies and gentlemen, your host Diamond, David Lee Roth!"* David Lee then busts into the room, grabbed the mic and yelled, *"Let's dance!"* 'Get Down Tonight' by KC and The Sunshine Band started to play. David starts to dance around the room with many different women. The disco ball was lit up and shooting a light show everywhere. I literally could not believe what was going on. After his little dance he exited the room without a word. His road manager then came up to us and asked who we were. Jesse and I introduced ourselves as the lead singer and guitar player of *Jackyl*. The road manager then said we were the right guys and David wanted to meet us. We walked back to the room David was in, to see him sitting down in a small, dark, and weird room with a few drinks on the table. The first thing he said was, *"John Kalodner told me to say hello to you boys."* We said we were big fans and everything. David was extremely nice and when we were about to leave he extended his arm like Jesus Christ himself and said, *"I hope you go to the heavens."* A great musician wishing my career great success was amazing but one thing really stuck with me. After I shook his hand I could not get over the fact that his hand was the softest fucking thing I had ever felt. It was literally softer than a baby's ass. After we walked back to the car, Jesse and I were in shock. When we finally started talking we talked about how soft those hands were. He must have never even picked up a pen. It was surreal.

<> <> <>
Gary Busey – A.K.A Nick Nolte

It has always been funny to me when someone mixes up celebrities and calls them by the wrong name. This story takes place around 1993/94. We were on tour with Damn Yankees. Damn Yankees were made up of Ted Nugent (of Ted Nugent* we'll get to Ted later), Jack Blades (of Night Ranger), and Tommy Shaw (of Styx), and Michael Cartellone (of Lynyrd Skynyrd). This super group was the brain child of the great John Kalodner. Being one of our first big tours, it exposed us to a lot of celebrities. My brother, still to this day, cannot get a celebrity's name right. We were playing in Radio City Music Hall in New York. In this story, my brother came up to me and said there was a famous actor in the Damn Yankees' dressing room. He said, *"You know who he is. You know him. You like him. You think he's killer!"* I asked him, *"Who is it?"* Chris thought for a second and spits out *"It's Nick Nolte! It's Nick Nolte!"* I am a fan of Nick Nolte so I quickly followed him to the dressing rooms. When we got there, we made our way through the crowd and once they parted we ran up to "Nick Nolte" and Chris said, *"Hey I would like you to meet my brother, Jeff. Jeff, meet Nick Nolte."* The man turned to me, extended his hand to shake, and said *"Hey Jeff, I'm Gary Busey."* I couldn't contain my laughter. I had to quickly get the hell out of there because I was laughing so hard. Chris wasn't embarrassed because that's the way we are. I left to go to my dressing room in order to laugh in privacy. Speaking of Ted...

<> <> <>
Ted Nugent/Damn Yankees

I love Ted Nugent. Some people slam him but screw 'em all. Ted is who he is 100% of the time no matter what. He doesn't back down from any of his beliefs and stands up for what he believes in. He is a true American patriot and no one can deny it. So here goes the story of us meeting Ted.

We were out playing, trying to get a record deal when we got a call from a friend of Jesse Dupree's asking if we wanted to open for Ted Nugent on his famous Whiplash Bash tour. All of the shows were in Michigan starting in Flint and ending on New Year's Eve at Cobo Hall in Detroit. Cobo Hall is one of the most famous venues for rock in the country where all of my heroes have played. This is where KISS recorded their 'KISS ALIVE' album and Bob Seger recorded his 'Live Bullet' record. So it's a magical place. But on this occasion we didn't have any money so we had to rent a van and drive from Atlanta to Flint, Michigan pulling our gear behind us. So we made it to Flint and played our first shows in front of 20,000 people. The funny thing was after two days we barely saw Ted to thank him for having us. Another thing about Ted is he is an absolute family man. We couldn't believe he actually drove himself and his family from show to show in one of his personal SUV's.

On the third morning out we were loading up in our van to go to the next show when we saw Ted's family getting in to their SUV. Suddenly, Ted exits the hotel and heads right towards our rental van. I have to tell you, I was scared. Half out of respect, half because Ted always has a gun and Chris was talking to his daughter the night before. As Ted walked towards our car I said, *"Holy shit here comes Ted!"* I rolled down the window quickly and he said, *"Jackyl boys, follow me. I'm taking y'all to breakfast."* I heaved a sigh of relief. So off we go to the closest Denny's with Ted Nugent.

When you go out with Ted, people tend to stare. We sat down at a table and instantly Ted started to order for everyone. Not just for his family but for us too. We didn't know what to do. But at that moment we understood it was Ted's way or no way. We would be eating our fried mush. I felt honored because it was just us (*Jackyl*), Ted, and Ted's family. We ate what he ordered. It was hilarious. But make no mistake, I have been playing guitar since I was 14 and I can tell you Ted Nugent is one of the best guitar players I have ever seen. He is a master of everything he does; music, hunting, and talking. He is a harsh, straight up guy, but like I said he is 100% honest. We were young and filled with piss and vinegar. He loved that about us. He said he saw a lot of himself in us. That would pump us up to go on stage and kick fucking ass. After our set, we were leaving the stage and Ted said to me, *"That was pretty good but you boys better take note of this tonight."* Then he went on stage and blew the place away. After the show he would always ask, *"Didn't I play great tonight?"* That's the thing about Ted; he would talk a mountain of trash but then back it up. If you can back it up then you deserve to talk as much trash as you can.

About 18 months after our awesome tour with Ted, we reunited with Nugent at Rumbo Recorders. We were recording our first record and the Damn Yankees were recording their second record. This story taught me a lot about the world.

One day while recording, Ted busted into our studio and said, *"Worley boys, come with me!"* We followed him out to the parking lot and we saw a Ryder truck pulling up outside of Rumbo Recorders. When the truck opened up, we started to unload fake deer, bear, and elk into the parking lot. Being in California this started a huge commotion around the studio. We already had animal cruelty groups on our ass because on 'The Lumberjack' song they found out we had real chickens in the studio. How they found out I have no idea. In order to get those real chickens we had to bring them into the studio with real hay, turning it into a barn and causing a huge mess. So while we were unloading Ted's practice targets someone at the studio must have called the record company saying that we were setting up real animals to kill with a bow and arrow. Eventually through the grape vine, John Kalodner heard of this stunt and called us on speaker phone. He first asked us if anyone else was in the room. We said no and then he said, *"This is great. Whatever you guys are doing, keep doing it. This publicity is awesome!"* Jesse then asked, *"What about all of the other people at the studio?"* Kalodner screams back, *"Fuck those people!"* We all laughed our asses off. I remembered Ted's best piece of advice that he gave us that we try to follow in every show we can. *"Never play your whole set. So if you had an hour to play, you gotta play 50 minutes and make them wish you played longer."* We also learned the term 'to baste in it" which means to stay just a little bit longer in the spotlight. I will never be able to repay Ted Nugent for all of his advice and inspiration. His tutoring taught me how to survive 20 years in the music business. The Whiplash Bash tour led to our first big tour with The Damn Yankees.

<><><>

THE AEROSMITH STORIES
The Marlboro Man

This story happened during Aerosmith's "Pumped" tour. This was our second big tour. Being out with The Damn Yankees was one thing but touring with a band of Aerosmith's stature was incredible. At this point we thought that we had to party our asses off to keep up with the big shots. Little did we know that they had to keep clean like altar boys.

The first show of the tour was in 1994 in Topeka, Kansas. In those days Aerosmith would take up and coming bands out to play in front of tens of thousands of fans for a few weeks to get some major exposure. Aerosmith let everyone get their chance, but we really lucked up after our three weeks. Megadeth took over where we left off but it didn't work out. So on our way home we got a call from Aerosmith asking us to finish their entire tour. The rumor was Dave Mustaine talked trash on the radio about Aerosmith. Joe Perry heard about it and fired them on the spot. So we got to open for Aerosmith for the rest of the tour.

Rumor also had it that Megadeth found out they were fired when they went to eat at a Denny's on the morning of their first show with Aerosmith. The waitress came up to them and said,

"Hey you must be Jackyl." Someone in Megadeth said, *"No, we're Megadeth. We're on tour with Aerosmith."* The waitress then informed them, *"No you're not. The radio said Megadeth wasn't playing with Aerosmith and Jackyl had taken their place."* This goes to show you it can happen to the best of 'em. So, back to Aerosmith.

To let you know what it was like, Aerosmith's drug and alcohol counselors hounded us to make sure we didn't have any intoxicants around the band. They had to keep the band clean because so many people depended on them being able to play and do shows. Aerosmith is a money making machine. This story is called The Marlboro Man because one of the drug and alcohol counselors looked just like the classic Marlboro cowboy that was in the old Marlboro cigarette advertisements. He had the iconic Marlboro man mustache and a deathly stare. It was rumored that he was an ex-DEA agent. Anytime we would go near ANY of the guys in Aerosmith, the Marlboro Man would grab our drinks and smell them for alcohol.

One thing I will never forget was on our first day back during Aerosmith's sound check, Joe and Steven began to fight about what songs that would be on the set list. No one was in the room but me, Aerosmith, and some crew guys. Joe and Steven have an interesting relationship. They were the only two that could tell each other to "fuck off". No one else in the world was allowed to say that. So after our set the first night back, the entire Aerosmith band came into our dressing room. They welcomed us back and gave us a gift, a huge stereo! I still remember Steven Tyler saying, *"You boys aren't making enough noise so we got you this."* We had a few issues on our first three weeks but we didn't want to bring up any problems. We were lucky to be there. We didn't say a word until Tom Hamilton, the bass player for Aerosmith, said, *"So guys you're here for the rest of the tour, what can we do to make it better?"* We told them our situation of no sound checks and 15 minute sets. We also said it would be nice if we got better parking because we had to park 2 miles from the gig. When you're that big, even your *road crew* thinks they're rock stars. The guys in Aerosmith had no idea this was happening. I personally mentioned my annoyance with their hall monitor, The Marlboro Man. I told them of the drink sniffing. I went as far as saying, *"I think he's just one step away from a full cavity search."* The guys laughed to each other and the only thing Tom Hamilton said about it was, *"We'll take care of it."* The next day it was 100% different. The Marlboro Man greeted us at the next gig with a smile and was directing us into a parking spot right next to the back door of the show. He also informed us that we had a 45 minute set and that we had a minimum of 20 minutes for a sound check. You have to understand, even though we were opening for them every single night, we never saw them because they showed up 5 minutes before they played. Back then we were so poor we had to play little shitty venues just to make enough money to be able to open for Aerosmith. We would only make $500 a night but got a shit load of free publicity. So two nights before we opened for one of the biggest rock bands in the world, we would play in some hole in the wall club for enough money to survive.

Watching Aerosmith play almost every day for months on end really taught me how to survive in the rock business. They truly are a class act and it doesn't take a lot to understand why they are in the Rock Hall of Fame. It was like getting a rock education at Harvard.

<><><>

Peter Fonda / John "Paul Mitchell" DeJoria

Around 2006/07 we were headlining the 100th anniversary of Harley Davidson celebration in Milwaukee, WI. Also at this show, musicians like Toby Keith, Ted Nugent, and Kid Rock were there. We were all playing in honor of the great motorcycle company. Before our show, we were sitting back stage and once again (as if it's some screwed up theme) my brother comes in to our dressing room and says, *"Guess who's coming in here?"* I said, *"Who?"* Chris said, *"Peter Fonda and some guy that you know but I can't think of his name. And they have four Playboy centerfold models with them!"* I said, *"You're full of shit!"* Chris responded with, *"Look!"* We all jump to see if this is true. Damn Chris was right. Peter Fonda, John Paul DeJoria (The Paul of Paul Mitchell and the owner of Patron Tequila), and four gorgeous girls came into our backstage area. We were floored. We did our introductions and started talking. As soon as we start talking I knew Peter Fonda was either really fucked up or so cool he could barely breathe. He was talking very slowly and had a smile glued to his face that I was not familiar with. After we chatted a bit, John Paul came over. Trying to break the ice, I asked John Paul, *"Was it the Patron or the hair products that got you the women?"* John Paul laughed. Jesse asked Peter Fonda, *"Hey man, would Peter Fonda, "Easy Rider" do us the honor of introducing us on stage tonight?"* (Easy Rider is a famous movie with Jack Nickelson that started the drug biker culture in the 60's) Peter asked, *"What do you want me to say?"* Jesse said, *"You're Peter Fonda you can say whatever you want!"* He very slowly agreed and I think *"Kick ass!"*

Right before the show, my road manager placed 6 chairs on my side of the stage where John Paul, Peter Fonda, and 4 gorgeous Playboy girls would watch the show. The lights went down and our intro started to play as Peter Fonda goes shuffling out to the microphone. Picking up the mic, Fonda starts to trail off very awkwardly. *"Good evening everyone."* The place explodes! *"I want to welcome everyone and... welcome this band to play tonight and..."* He continues to ramble on about shit we have no idea about. The intro had to be replayed as he continued to ramble. Eventually we couldn't wait any longer so Jesse just hits it. We start to play and Peter Fonda is slightly startled at this explosion of energy. He finally wobbled back to his seat on the side of the stage as we finished our first song. I start the second song and here comes Fonda again. We were thinking '*What the fuck?*' as Peter aimlessly meanders all over the stage. Our stage manager would have thrown his ass off of the stage into the crowd if it weren't Peter Fucking Fonda! Then, John Paul pops up and gently takes Fonda by the arm and leads him back to his seat. I really can't make this shit up! This was happening before my eyes. A famous billionaire led a legendary movie star back to his seat like the father of an unruly child. There were no more incidents and we finished our set. As we were leaving the stage, there was a truck ramp for all of our equipment and if you jumped on the middle of the ramp it would launch you like a diving board. I think it was the opening band standing by our stage wanting to high five us. Roman Glick, our bass player, had different plans for them. Let me tell you this, never high-five Roman Glick. You've been warned. Running directly down the ramp, he yelled "Easy Rider!" Roman jumps as hard as he could onto the ramp and launched himself right onto two of the opening band members. Both of Roman's shoulders hit each of the men directly in the chest, knocking the wind out of them and taking them to the ground. I was laughing my ass off on the stage. Both guys were knocked sideways like bowling pins and Roman did a Jackie Chan style roll to his feet.

Without a word Roman runs into the dressing room, leaving me with the mess. All of our guests stared in horror at the scene in front of them. That kind of insanity has never been seen since Iggy Pop told the crowd to fuck off in the middle of his show. I went to the dressing room to laugh my fucking ass off. That was our hilarious ending to the 100th anniversary of Harley Davidson in Milwaukee, Wisconsin.

<> <> <>

Brian May - We (Jackyl) ... Are the Champions

Right after we got our first record deal, we were playing in a club in Atlanta. In those days we were on fire and packing in the crowds. On this particular night, before we went on stage, my buddy, who works for a record company doing promotions called us and said, *"Hey put me on the guest list. I'm bringing Brian May (lead guitarist of Queen) to watch the show."* I couldn't believe it, I didn't believe it! And I wouldn't believe it! But no shit, as soon as the spot lights hit the stage I could see the outline of Brian May's curly hair standing next to our sound man at the sound board. I almost shit on myself. We killed it that night. Then, we get word that Brian wanted to meet us. We of course invite him back. The only way I could describe Brian May is that he is an eloquent gentleman. Not only is he one of the best guitarist in my opinion and my favorite guitarist, but he is the nicest guy imaginable. He said that we were great and he loved our rock energy. I asked him about all of his famous licks and how he played them. Can you imagine Jeff Worley back stage talking about guitars with Brian May? Near the end of our conversation he made the comment that has stuck with me to this day. Brian May said, *"You know, Freddie would have loved you guys."* Brain giggled, *"He would have especially loved that song 'She Loves My Cock'."* I went back to my hotel and thought about the night. At the moment I am writing this (and I'm sure for years to come), this is the best compliment I have ever gotten. To me, it is a real badge of honor.

<> <> <>

Maiden Rules

Note: The guys in Maiden wouldn't want me to say this but I'm going to say it anyway. Iron Maiden is one of the best bands in the fucking world... PERIOD!

<> <> <>

Paul Di'Anno

From a personal perspective, these chapters on Iron Maiden hit home for me. I am a huge fan of Iron Maiden and their style strongly influenced my musical career. In 1981, Paul Di'Anno left Iron Maiden and was replaced by Bruce Dickinson. After that Di'Anno formed a new band by the name of Battlezone. I didn't really know who Bruce Dickinson was at that time but I knew Paul Di'Anno was the singer on Iron Maiden 'Killers' record/world tour. It so happened that Battlezone was playing only an hour's drive away from my home town. As soon as I got word Paul Di'Anno's Battlezone was playing so close I had to open for them. With a lot of smooth talking and begging I think we agreed to open for them if we unloaded all of their gear and we would play for free. This was around 1986. Paul Di'Anno liked us so much that he wanted to hang around the next night to watch us play at another club in town. This was the beginning of a disaster.

My father had come up to watch us play the next night and was exposed to the hardcore mentality of Paul Di'Anno and his crew. My pop also brought along his girlfriend at the time. We were all hanging around having some drinks when all of a sudden the drummer from Battlezone unzipped his pants and flopped his uncircumcised penis on my future step-mom's shoulder. This wasn't a brief brushing of the penis. He put his member on her shoulder and let it lay there. Everyone was shocked. My dad started to flip out and asked if it was going to ruin my career if he cut his dick off. I hurried up to Paul and said, *"Hey, your drummer's dick is on my dad's girlfriend's shoulder and my pop told me he was going to cut it off if he didn't get the hell out of here."* Paul was totally cool about the situation and said, *"Hell! Tell him to kick his ass! Tell him to cut his dick off! The pervert deserves it!"* Whew! Luckily, he had relocated his junk and disappeared into the crowd.

Later on I witnessed the same drummer taking the light bulbs out of the sockets and pissing into them, just for the shock. Not the shock value, the actual electrical shock. These guys were drinking the cheapest vodka they had like water. When that wasn't enough for him, he would stick his entire *uncircumcised* phallus right into the bulb socket with the power on. This would singe the tip of his dick and give him a sexual thrill, I guess. I thought this was extremely bizarre but also extremely hilarious, making me laugh my damn ass off. I never saw that drummer again and I never planned to. I was recently told that he had once played for a New Jersey thrash band called Overkill. I'm just glad nothing happened between him and my dad. I would have had to identify that penis in a line up just like in the movie Porkys!

<> <> <>

Bruce Dickinson

Fast forward ten years from the 'dick on the shoulder' incident. Our second record 'Push Comes to Shove' had just come out and we were heading out on our first big headlining tour. The lineup would be the guitarist Richie Kotzen. Richie had just gotten fired from Poison for stealing the drummer's wife. Richie is now in the band The Winery Dogs. After Richie it was Bruce Dickinson, the legendary Iron Maiden singer. At that point he was working on his solo career with his album 'Balls to Picasso'. The fact that Bruce Dickinson (who replaced Paul Di'Anno and the man in my opinion made Iron Maiden what it is) was opening up for us floored me. I was learning many lessons in the music business. First off, if you stay around long enough a band will always have its ups and downs. It also taught me that you must be confident in your own ability but always be humble because you never know what will happen next, just like with Bruce.

Let me tell you a little story about Bruce Dickinson. Everyone now knows about Bruce being a pilot. This just shows he's not just a dumb ass musician. On that tour, he would fly a Cessna to every show. One specific incident that I remember on this tour stays with me til today.

We were in Lincoln, Nebraska playing a show for the local radio station. We had the same line up except for the addition of the legendary southern rock band BlackFoot. If you're not familiar, BlackFoot had some huge hits in the 70's and 80's like

'Train, Train' and 'Highway Song'. To this day, if you turn on classic rock radio you will hear these songs in regular rotation. Their lead singer was our old friend Ricky Medlocke. At this point, instead of being in a tour bus he was riding in a van pulling a trailer. So we had Ricky on the bus just chilling and chatting. About 10 minutes into our conversation there was a knock at the bus door. I looked out the window and say, *"It's Bruce Dickinson!"* Ricky said, *"Bruce! We opened up for Maiden on their 'Number of the Beast' tour in Europe! Bring him on the bus. I want to say hey."* So I walked over and opened the door. Before I could say anything Bruce said in his classic English accent, *"Jeff me son, if it's not too much trouble could I borrow a spot of jam?"* I said to Bruce in my southern accent, *"You mean jelly?"* He laughed and said, *"Precisely, that would be brilliant."* I invited him on the bus. As soon as Bruce saw Ricky, Ricky said, *"You've got to be shitting me!"* These guys hadn't seen each other in a long time and they had an awesome reunion right in front of me. I was in heaven. I had two colossal musicians reminiscing about playing in mega stadiums right there on my bus. That showed me my most important lesson, spending time with these guys proved to me those who are at the top, those who have survived decades, were there for a reason. A shark is at the top of the food chain not because he is lucky but because he is smart, respectable, and bad fucking ass. Not only did they rock the damn house, everyone and their mother knew who Iron Maiden was.

A few years after this, Ricky Medlocke joined Lynyrd Skynyrd and tours with them to this day. Bruce, as we all know, returned to Iron Maiden. Now, instead of flying Cessna's to the shows, he flies Ed Force One, Iron Maiden's personal 747. Let me tell you something, even if you are not a fan of Iron Maiden, you have to respect them. You can go find an unknown tribe in the South American rainforest, or witness the first alien landing on earth and see a t shirt with Iron Maiden's "The Trooper" on it.

<> <> <>

Jim Dandy

I had heard of Black Oak Arkansas from my cool hippie uncle when I was very young. I didn't really 'get it' but they were something my uncle would listen to. So when we first came out (the early 1990's) people were constantly comparing us to Black Oak Arkansas. Don't get me wrong, I wasn't offended but after listening to some of their records and after making our first record I just could not see the connection. The only comparison I could see was their lead singer was a good looking guy back in the day with long hair just like Jesse Dupree.

We were on tour and it brought us to Memphis, TN. We didn't know it yet but that's where Jim "Dandy" Mangrum had been living for a while. Half-jokingly we had mentioned to our road manager that if Jim Dandy of Black Oak Arkansas showed up to our show we would give him some passes and welcome him in. After a few days went by we found out Jim Dandy had somehow heard of his invitation and he called our office. The phone call went like this: (if you don't know, Jim Dandy's voice sounds like a cross between Mongolian Tuvian Throat Singing and a buzz saw) : *"UH YEEAAHHH this is Jim Daaaandyyyyy from Black Oak. I know you boys were inviting me to your show so I'm just calling ahead to say I'm gonna need a couple of passes and I need to park near the buses. See you in a few days."* We made sure he got what he needed. Sure enough Jim Dandy showed up later that night with a date. The woman was a bleach-blonde stripper in her late sixties with somewhere in the neighborhood of HHH sized titties. We were all in our dressing room chilling out before the show. Sitting around with some drinks, Jim Dandy took out a tiny bit of cocaine and asked, *"Y'all don't mind if I do a little bump? Ain't never hurt nobody."* To me it was a funny thing to say and we didn't give a damn so we said sure. We were shocked when Jim Dandy laid out two big lines for him and his lady friend and proceeded to snort up all of the coke in one go without offering us any. If Jim Dandy asked me to do a line with him I would have said yes for rock n' roll sake. Some guys were pissed. Personally I thought it was fucking hilarious.

A few months after the 'Bogart of Blow' incident, Black Oak Arkansas was playing not too far from my hometown. I was off of the road and I decided to go see them. The venue was only what I can describe as a barren field. Comparably, the county fair would be considered the Madison Square Garden. Black Oak's 'dressing room' was what looked like a cracked out ruin of a building. It didn't even have a roof. I felt really bad for them at that point. After standing bored out of my mind in this field watching cover bands Jim Dandy finally got on stage. I'm not making fun of him but I have to describe his attire. He was wearing golden spandex pants and moccasins in the middle of the summer. It must have been 105. It was a sight you cannot UN-see. Sweet, sweet, Connie must have left one cock unsucked because either Jim Dandy's penis is gargantuan or he jammed one of Ted Nugent's bear sausages down his pants! But I must say he's a survivor. In 2014, I pulled every string with Jesse and Mike Ballard to get Jim Dandy and his new version of Black Oak Arkansas on stage at The Full Throttle. That night at the Throttle, I tried to get all of my friends to go up on stage in order to view Jim Dandy's large dangle. I had a single taker, my friend Fireplug, and I think he has pictures!

<><><>

Ali!... I call him Clay! He Clay to me. I say Clay

My Mohammed Ali/Cassius Clay (whichever you prefer) story is not an actual meeting. It was more of a sighting. A few years back, the band and I were flying to Minneapolis St. Paul from Atlanta for a show. We found out we couldn't upgrade our seats so in protest we decided to get drunk at the airport bar. While throwing drinks back we saw a commotion near the gate for our flight. Being Atlanta it was a normal sight. A large shuttle was beeping loudly while a large mob was following it. Not really giving a damn we continued drinking. When it was time to board the plane we got on and walked past first class. The seats that would have been ours were taken by Mohammed Ali and his family! We were in awe. The sad part about it was "The Champ" was showing some bad signs of Parkinson's, so we shuffled back to our seats.

After the flight we headed to baggage claim. We actually passed Ali and his entourage and I stopped to ask them if we could take a picture with him. His wife was really nice but said she would rather not. If she let us take a picture then others would come and bombard them. We of course respected their wishes and left them alone. As our roadies got all of our gear and we sat outside at the pickup area, we looked over to see the great Mohammed Ali just sitting on a bench by himself with his walker. No caretakers or wife around. I turned to Roman, our bassist, and say *"Hey I'm going to get this picture."* We giggled and I walked casually near the great boxer. The bench he was sitting at allowed for access around it so someone could walk behind it. I walked behind Ali then posed for the camera. Roman snapped the pic and no one was the wiser. I do have the picture, but once again out of respect for the legend, I am keeping it out of this book.

<><><>

Five Seconds of Greatness and That Sweet Muskrat Love

We recorded our first record at a famous studio called Rumbo Recorders in Canoga Park, CA (You will read many stories of Rumbo in this book) Rumbo, at that time was owned by the legendary Captain and Tennille, the singing duo. If you're not familiar, they were a 70's super group that consisted of a lady singer and some guy that looked like Gopher off of the TV show The Love Boat. They had such hits as 'Love Will Keep Us Together', 'Do That to Me One More Time', and my band's particular favorite 'Muskrat Love'. Not only did The Captain and Tennille record their hits there, other famous people recorded there as well such as Guns N Roses, Kiss, Spinal Tap, and *Jackyl*. It gives me chills every time I say I made my first record in the same place they recorded 'This is Spinal Tap'. We had been in a few recording studios but nothing of this magnitude. When we got there we learned it was actually three recording studios in one building. Here's how small the world is. The Damn Yankees with our Uncle Ted was in one studio, we were in one studio, and The Traveling Wilburys were in the third studio. If you are not familiar with the Traveling Wilburys they were Tom Petty, Roy Orbinson, Jeff Lynne of Electric Light Orchestra, Bob Dylan, and some fella named George Harrison. (Apparently he was in a little band back in 60's called The Beatles) At first we didn't really see the Traveling Wilburys but we could smell them, in a good way. It smelled like a Cheech and Chong convention. The funny thing was our producer, Brenden O'Brian had warned us of any drug use. Brenden said if he saw any drug use in the studio he was gone. We took that to heart. After sneaking little joints around the studio I was finally caught. I thought we were absolutely done and we might have lost our record deal. Brenden looked at me and said, *"You idiot! You can smoke all the weed you want. What I meant was doing lines of coke off of the mixing board or shooting heroin in the bathroom. This studio costs y'all $2,500 a day. It's coming out of your money if you sell any records in the first place."* Talk about tough love! None of us had hard drugs in mind anyway. We couldn't afford them if we did. We just wanted to smoke a little pot and play music. The guys from the Traveling Wilburys were smoking the best weed I have ever smelled.

Being in LA and in this environment for the first time I had never really seen such famous people before. One day, coming back from lunch, we pulled up to the studio in our last remaining piece of shit Dodge K car. In the studio parking lot sat two identical bad ass Mercedes-Benz convertibles. You could tell they were rentals because they were exactly the same model, color, and interiors. After seeing these sweet cars for a second I opened the door to the studio and was face to face with Jeff Lynne and George Harrison. I was in shock. All I could do was put up my hand and say, *"Hey."* They both responded in a strange unison, *"Aye mate."* back to me casually and went out to the parking lot. I froze. I watched the two legends get into their Mercedes and drive off. All was one with the world! This image was etched into my brain and has been a go-to motivation for my career. Here's how I looked at it. There I was in my shitty rental car that I was sharing with 8 other dudes while those guys went off in their own Mercedes. Which they fully deserved. From then on I had a different mindset. I walked back into that studio and played my ass off. Now it was serious.

Oh yeah by the way, I failed to mention that every Friday Captain and Tennille would come by the studio to collect massive amounts of cash. My unprofessional medical opinion is that The Captain had some sort of social anxiety. Tennille would come inside for the money and The Captain stayed with the ship. One day my brother Chris was getting equipment from the front of the studio. From the supply cabinet you could view the parking lot. Chris ran back to the studio and said, *"Hey, The Captain is out in the parking lot!"* I ran outside to see.

Looking out into the parking lot all I saw an empty car. *"Chris, you're full of shit!"* I said. Chris said, *"Go up and look in that car."* I casually walked towards the car. When I got close enough I saw him slouched very low in the car with his captain's hat on. I think when I walked closer he slouched even more. Chris also had another run in with the Captain. While fetching more gear from the supply cabinet, he discovered the Captain's hide out. Yes, a grown ass man just chilling in a closet. I don't know how to explain it but it's true story.

<><><>

Totally Pauly

A few days after the Jeff Lynne and George Harrison incident, the Traveling Wilburys had finished their recording and were out. Their studio space was occupied by Vince Neal, the singer for Motley Crue. Vince was doing a soundtrack for a movie called 'Encino Man' which starred Brenden Fraiser, Sean Astin, and Pauly Shore. On that day Pauly was at Rumbo while we were there. He was interviewing bands for his MTV show called 'Totally Pauly'. After interviewing Vince Neal and The Damn Yankee's, Pauly thought it was good idea to enter the *Jackyl's* den. I'm pretty sure Uncle Ted sent him down to us because number 1, I'm sure he had never heard of us, number 2 Uncle Ted knew exactly what was going to happen. It just happened to be one of the days that we were recording 'The Lumberjack'. That means that we had the chainsaw out. After talking to us for a minute, I could tell Pauly was a little on edge just because of our southern roughness. We also had a shit load of guns with us but that's another story. As we're listening to some of the stuff we had just recorded, Jesse busts into the room with the chainsaw. As soon as Jesse cranked that son of a bitch up, Pauly Shore snapped his head in the direction of the noise. Obviously a chainsaw revving in a small room is loud as fuck! I then held up my Gibson Les Paul and Jesse carved MTV JACKYL on the back of the guitar. I don't even know if Pauly said good bye. We looked around and he was fucking out of there! It was hilarious.

Fast-forward about 10 years later, we were headlining the AVN Awards (adult movies) at Caesar's Palace. We always love being in Vegas, but if you have us headlining the Porn Awards crazy shit is bound to happen. That night was literally when dynamite and moonshine collided. Who was hosting the awards show but none other than legendary porn star Ron Jeremy and our friend Pauly Shore. When Pauly found out we were playing there he seemed to be having a constant panic attack. He literally walked all the way around the auditorium just to avoid us. I felt bad that we scared him so much because we never really did anything to him. It is still hilarious, to me at least, that we can scare one guy for so long.

< > < > < >
HALL OF FAMERS
Brian Johnson

The legendary Brian Johnson, the man who replaced Bonn Scott in AC/DC, is one of my heroes and I have always wanted to meet him. Not only did that happen but he actually recorded a song called 'Locked 'n Loaded' with us back in 1997 on our Cut the Crap record. He also co-wrote 'Kill the Sunshine' on our 2004 Relentless record. This is a story that shows how fate had intervened with us again. The story goes like this...

Jesse had gotten a call from a lady in Florida asking if he would fly down to sing a few songs for a charity show in Tampa. After a few questions Jesse found out that lady was none other than Brenda Johnson, wife of AC/DC's Brian Johnson. Brenda had also said her husband was going to be there as well. As soon as Jesse found that out he said, *"Hell yeah I'll be down there!"* At the charity event Jesse sang a song with Brian. They hit it off and Jesse came back to Atlanta with some news for us. He told us that Brian Johnson was going to come up and stay in Atlanta and work on a song with us. At first we thought Jesse was fucking with us. I told him to quit fooling around because I didn't believe him. All Jesse said was, *"You'll see!"* But no shit Brian Johnson came up. He is one of the coolest people you could ever meet we were working on a song called 'Locked 'n Loaded' and at that time we didn't think he was going to actually record with us. We thought he was there to give us some pointers. But when Jesse started to sing the song Brian stopped him and showed him how to sing it a certain way. Then Brian said, *"Play it from the top."* and he told Jesse to do the first verse and he would do the second. They traded off for the entire song and my God it sounded great. We stopped after that take because we were tired. We had been drinking and it couldn't get any better. Mike Fraser, our producer, told us confidentially that AC/DC doesn't record anything outside of the band. Malcom and Angus Young wouldn't have any of it.

The next morning we listened to the track and it was even better than the night before. We all looked at each other and I said, *"That needs to be the song."* Brian said, *"I think you're right."* Fraser asked him what Malcom and Angus would say. Brian said he'd take care of it and that was that. What started as just one night of recording turned into three awesome nights of fun.

One morning, Brian got up and cooked us a traditional English breakfast. It consisted of extremely runny eggs, pork & beans, and English breakfast sausage. I usually only eat my eggs well done but hey, these were cooked by Brian Johnson so I drank them like a good boy. While Brian exposed us to an English breakfast, we introduced him to the iconic American Taco Bell. It was hard for us to even imagine Brian had never heard of the fast food place. When we walked into Taco Bell, everyone stared at us. At the ordering counter he asked me, *"What do I order me sons?"* We told him to get the beef burritos because they were pretty much meat and cheese. He ordered it and we all sit down to eat. Brain looked at the burrito and said in his funny as hell English accent, *"I don't know what end to bite."* Then Brian takes one big bite, looks at me very concerned, and said, *"Me boy! This is terrible and it's drier than a nun's cunt!"* We explode with laughter! I am going to go on record and say this was the first and last time he ate at Taco Bell. Not only could he rock the fucking house, Brian could be a comedian and also sing just like Frank Sinatra. He also knows everything about World War II and military history. We talked at great length about his days in the British Air Borne.

After Brian left, we were on pins and needles while waiting on the news of 'Locked 'n Loaded'. Finally we got word from Malcom and Angus. Brian called us and repeated what they said, *"It sucks, but it sucks less than the rest of the bullshit that is coming out so I guess it can stay."* That was another massive compliment about my work. What they meant was '*no one is better than AC/DC but your shit is better than everyone other than us.*' When our album 'Cut the Crap' was released, as expected 'Locked 'n Loaded' was climbing up the rock charts so Brian would come out to jam with us at live shows. We were invited back to play at the Live Stock Festival in Tampa, Florida. This would be our second time at that festival and we all hoped it would go a little smoother than the first time. (Remember the Vietnam flashback) We called Brian Johnson to see if he would like to play with us. He said sure, just to pick him up at his house in Sarasota and we'd ride together on our tour bus to the show.

We followed Brian's directions to his house and it led us to a massive gated community. Just when you think you know rich, you see this neighborhood. They let us through the gate and we got lost in this maze of ridiculous wealth. Eventually we drove by this little old lady that was wearing a fur coat, covered in expensive jewelry and walking a poodle. Our driver rolled down the window. Before we could ask her for directions, she blurted out, "*Oh you must be looking for Brian's house.*" This nice old lady directed us to the rock legend's house. Most wealthy people might have a three or four car garage but Brian had a ten car garage. That was just at his house. Most of his car collection was kept in a warehouse down the road. I won't waste time listing all of the insane cars he had but there was some serious cash sunk into his collection.

When we pulled up to his house we saw him standing on his front lawn directing the bus where to park. We had some time to kill and Brian invited us in. Brian's wife had made a ton of food and Brian told us, "*My house is your house.*" He meant that. He took me through his bedroom and to his personal gym to work out. Anyone can say 'make yourself at home', Brian Johnson truly meant it. I told him I felt bad for using all of his personal things. He said, "*Oh me son, I bloody paid for it we're gonna use it.*" We all had showers and ate some food and explored his amazing house. We even had a drink in his legendary English pub, an exact replica of a pub you would find in England. It had stained glass doors that were decorated with the two cannons from the album 'For Those About to Rock'. In the pub there was a huge bar with anything you could imagine to drink plus a picture of Brian with EVERYBODY. When I say *everybody*, I mean everyone from movie stars to race car drivers. As Brian was asking me what I wanted to drink I looked over at his wall. I was dumbfounded. It was covered with gold and platinum discs. Then out of the corner of my eye I saw it, a comically large record award for the album 'Back in Black'. I know that a diamond award in the United States is 10 million sales. This bad boy had sold 50 million copies. I don't even know what you call it. It brought me to my knees. Once again my life had changed and he became an extreme motivator for me. After we hung out for a little bit, we all loaded up on the bus and headed to the gig.

Motley Crue was headlining but not with Vince Neal. Neal parted ways with Motley Crue and singer John Corabi was his replacement. No one was there to see them. There was a lot of hype about us with Brian Johnson and the place was on fire. We opened our set as usual then Brian came out and sang 'Locked and Loaded'. Everyone fucking loved it! Then Brian and Jesse sang 'I Stand Alone'. We then played 'Back in Black' and I thought the crowd was going to lose their minds! That was the last song we were going to play but something in me made me hit the first lick of AC/DC's 'Shoot to Thrill'. The crowd erupted. Brian just looked at me and said in a Monty Python fashion, *"Jeff me son, I don't think I remember the words to the fucking song."* But he killed it anyway and it was fucking magic. Just like Vikings, we came into the venue, kicked everyone's ass and got the hell out of there before anyone could catch their breath. Now we don't usually leave a show that quickly and we always set aside time for a meet and greet with the fans to show our appreciation. This time however, Brian had to get back home because he was leaving the country the next morning. So we got the hell out ASAP! It was the first time we worked with a rock n' roll hall of famer but little did we know it wasn't going to be the last.

<><><>

Daryl McDaniels – The D from Run DMC

To this day I don't think the music world understands why one of the hip hop pioneers from Harlem would want to team up with a bunch of white boys from the south. Once again it must have been fate. Around 2010 we were working on our 'When Moonshine and Dynamite Collide' album. Most of the songs from the album were recorded but Jesse kept messing around with a song called 'Just Like a Negro' written by an old southern rock band by the name of Mothers Finest, which is a predominately black band. We, as a band, wanted to do a cover of it for our new album. Our only issue was that other people would think of us as racist just for saying the word negro. This pissed us off because not only are we not racist, the song Just Like a Negro was about paying respect to all black musicians of history.

We recorded our version of the music to the song and continued with our album. At that time Jesse was having a few rap artists in his studio recording their own stuff. Artists like Cee Lo Green had come by and word had gotten out about how nice 'Cock of the Walk' studio was. Eventually, Jesse got a call that Daryl McDaniels of Run DMC was in Atlanta and wanted to record there and this was when the magic started to happen.

Jesse approached Daryl about doing his own vocal track on 'Just Like a Negro' with us. He immediately loved the idea. We sent him the song and he asked for 16 bars. He recorded his part in New York and eventually he sent it back to us. Our first impression of the song was it was awesome. I was never nervous about the song because we didn't give a damn what other people thought of it. As far as I was concerned, this partnership was made by God. We broke down a lot of barriers with this song.

We brought together a southern rock band filled with white boys and a hard core, black, rap artist to honor the great black musicians of American history. Not only did he learn a lot from us, we learned a lot from him. We also created a great friendship that will last to the end of my days.

<><><>

Lynyrd Skynyrd

After all of the Lynyrd Skynyrd talk, we finally get to the story about how it all started. On our way back from California after recording our first record we got the call to stop in Texas somewhere for a gig opening for Lynryd Skynyrd. It didn't pay much and Skynyrd wasn't as 'hard' rock as we were but we were huge fans and jumped at the opportunity because it could lead to more shows.

Upon arrival to the venue our crew unloaded the gear. Lynyrd Skynyrd's road manger came right up to us and said, "*Look boys, what's the deal with the chainsaw?*" They must have heard about it and their road manager kindly asked us not to do it. His excuse was, "*You'll run Lynyrd Skynyrd's crowd off. They're leaning more country these days.*" I thought to myself, "*What's more country than a chainsaw?*" Chainsaw or not, I guess *Jackyl* was too much trouble for them. With no sound check we went on stage. The crowd just kind of stared at us, not knowing what to expect. We kicked ass though and at the end we had to break out the chainsaw. (In thousands of gigs, we've never played without it!) To our defense even the Skynyrd guys watched from the side of the stage and loved the chainsaw and the crowd ate it up. It was the only thing the crowd liked. After the show some of the guys from Lynyrd Skynyrd came into our dressing room and said, "*You guys were great, but we don't really mix and it's not going to work out.*" They were true gentlemen about it but very direct. I much prefer the direct route over pussy footing around. It was obvious that we were a hard rock band from the south and they were a southern rock band, two very different genres. The funny part is, later I found out that our road crew had raided their dressing room and ate all of their shrimp cocktail and drank all of their top shelf liquor. I completely understand why we didn't mix. Every time *Jackyl* played with Lynyrd Skynyrd we did something stupid. In our defense, we had to. You're a hard act to follow, Skynyrd.

< > < > < >

Buck Owens' Son/ Freddy Fender

This next story is going to show my age. When I was a kid, every Saturday night my family would religiously sit down and watch a show called "HEE-HAW". It was a "down home" country music variety show. It featured the day's top country music stars as guests alongside stupid hick jokes and skits. There were a bunch of women dressed just like Daisy Duke and the hosts were Roy Clark, guitarist extraordinaire and country legend Buck Owens. It was probably one of the longest running TV shows ever. I watched it my entire childhood so I knew the cast very well. It was a well-known rumor (spread by my father) that Buck Owens had sex with every female character on Hee-Haw. Years later, while touring in Bakersfield, California I found out that we were playing in Buck Owens' club. Our road manager came up to us at the gig and told us that the club was owned by Buck and run by his son Buddy. His son looked just like him and we thought it was funny in a very strange way. I had to go in and meet Buddy Owens. He did in fact look just like his father in a weird way. I had grown up with his father, just like him. I told him we were big fans of his dad's and were chatting him up. In Buddy's office there were pictures of every country star there was for the last 50 years. I pointed out a picture of Freddy Fender on the dressing room wall and told Buddy, *"I use to watch him on Hee-Haw, he was one of my dad's favorites."* Freddy was a well-known Mexican country singer. He was known for such hits as 'Wasted Days and Wasted Nights' and 'Before the Next Teardrop Falls'. Buddy Owens said, *"Hey if you like Freddy let's call him. He's feeling a little down and is in a bad way.* "Before we could say that wasn't necessary, Buddy had the phone ringing on speaker phone. A sad little man came onto the phone, *"Hellooo?"* Buddy said, *"Freddy, I've got some boys here that are big fans of yours.* I thought to myself, *"I never said we were fans."* From then on it was a very awkward conversation about how we watched him on Hee-Haw. It was like I was in the Twilight Zone. Other than that, the night was uneventful.

<> <> <>
Billy Gibbons, Touched by the Finger of God

Along with Brian May, Ted Nugent, and Joe Perry, Billy Gibbons is one of my top favorite guitarists. As I like to say, he is touched by the finger of God. One of my first albums that I owned was the 1973 ZZ Top "Fandango Live" album. The first side of the album was 30 minutes of blistering live rock while the other side was pure perfection in the studio. On the second side there were such hits as "Tush", "Blue Jean Blues", and my favorite "Nasty Dogs and Funky Kings". At the age of 10, just the titles blew my mind. Pretty much not a day goes by that I don't listen to something on that album.

<> <> <>
El Loco

In 1981 just after I graduated from high school, Jimmy Stiff and I went to see ZZ Top in Greenville, SC. They were on their El Loco tour. Those were the days of general admission so first come, first serve. From my Fandango record forward, I learned every lick Billy Gibbons had played. I've only said this a few times in my life but once again Billy Gibbons was touched by the finger of God. This means he doesn't have to think about playing in a godly fashion, he just does it.

So after their kick ass show, we wanted autographs but security wasn't having it. When we tried to walk into the back stage area we were kicked out immediately. We did not give up because we just had to meet Billy. On our second attempt we went full on James Bond. We crawled under the equipment truck and landed at security's feet. Not far from where we were lying, a limo was waiting for the rock stars. Just then ZZ Top comes out. We crawl out from the trailer and run over to them. Instantly security grabs our shirts and stops us in our tracks. I scream, *"Billy, can I get your autograph?"* Billy Gibbons put his hand out and says, *"Let 'em through, bring it up quick boys."* I got my autograph and we were out of there. We were the only ones to get autographs that night and it was not the last time we would meet some of our idols. My dream had come true; I had met my guitar idol. I had no idea our paths would cross again. (See the Most Memorable Gigs chapter for more ZZ Top)

<> <> <>

Jason Bonham

Jason Bonham is the son John Bonham, the drummer for Led Zeppelin, who had unfortunately died of alcohol related reasons. This is a sad story with a happy ending. It is ironic and a little sad that I met him while he was drunk in front of a club. The story goes like this...

In 1993, when we were recording our first record and went out to a club in LA. As I got out of our taxi I tripped over a guy half passed out on the curb. I turned him over and I noticed it was Jason Bonham! I helped him into the cab I got out of and off he went. Fast forward a year later. We were at another club in LA talking to Lemmy of Motorhead when I saw a guy and two women arguing with the bartender. I got closer to see Jason Bonham again, black out drunk. Lemmy said, *"That boy is going to kill himself just like his father if he doesn't slow down."* Lemmy had a lot of room to talk. I believe they stopped serving him and he was mad about it. Jason stumbled out in a drunken stupor. A couple of years after the last Jason Bonham sighting, the band Bonham were opening for couple of nights for our Push Comes to Shove tour. I was waiting for them to show up because I had 'met' Jason two times before but he had never really met me.

They showed up and I marched into his dressing room where he was already drinking. I'm not here to judge, the English like to drink just as much as us southern boys. He is a world class drummer and I hate to see anyone in pain like that. I've always said, *"There are people that party to have fun, and there's people that party because their life is not fun."* At that point, Jason wasn't having fun. I asked him, *"Hey Jason, do you remember me?"* He said, *"No but I love your band."* I had to explain to him that I stumbled over him on the street in Los Angles. One of his band mates said, *"Yeah that was him. We have to do it every night."* Now Jason is clean and is one of the best drummers in the business. Not because of his heritage but because of his skill. The man is a real survivor.

<> <> <>
Cheap Trick
A few years back we played at a big festival with the legendary band Cheap Trick. We were really excited and couldn't wait to play. During our show, Robin Zander and Rick Neilson were watching us. I like to throw picks to the crowd mostly because Rick Neilson was throwing picks to crowds before I could even pick up a guitar. After the show Robin and Rick walked off the stage with us. They both said that we kicked ass and they enjoyed the show. I told Rick that I was a massive fan. Rick said, *"I bet you are since you copied my pick throwing."* Robin Zander responded, *"Don't worry about him, you do it better and look better doing it."* I think that was a compliment. Then Robin Zander said, *"You know, they remind me of MC 5."* Rick said, *"You're right."* I did not know that was a compliment until later on in the bus when we looked them up on YouTube. I will leave it at this. Back in 1968, there was only one band screaming " MOTHER FUCKER" at you, it was MC 5.

<> <> <>
John Kalodner

John Kalodner is the man who made all of my dreams and some nightmares come true. Even before we were on his radar, we wanted the great Kalodner to sign us. When Jesse joined *Jackyl* and said he wanted to be signed by Kalodner also, we all got together and made our game plan. We knew that we needed the Jewish musical God that is John Kalodner. I *REALLY* wanted him to sign us. When we were playing little clubs Jesse would call out any guy with a beard. The spot light would hit the bearded man and Jesse would say, *"Let's give it up for John Kalodner."* The guy would be so confused but we were practicing for that faithful day. We eventually got a plan together to go to Los Angles and play some clubs to try to get noticed. This is a completely different story for a completely different book. I will tell you it turned out to be a cluster fuck and no one from any record company came out to see us. We had a long trip back home to Atlanta from Los Angles. We got back on a Sunday and on that next Tuesday we got a phone call. It was Jim Zumwalt. I've talked about Zummy already. He is an entertainment lawyer we knew from Nashville that was trying to help us get a deal.

Zumwalt said he got Kalodner to fly all the way to Atlanta to watch us play. Of course I did not believe a word of it. It wasn't because I thought Zumwalt was lying to me, it was because of our hard time in LA. You could literally see the record office buildings from the gigs we played but no one came out. We had a show booked that Friday in the middle of nowhere in Georgia in order to pay off a friend that bankrolled our LA trip. This venue was an old theater about 30 miles outside Atlanta and I had no faith that the musical master would even show up to a place like that. Here's the funny part. At that theater there was a two way mirror in our dressing room where we could see the crowd and had a great advantage point to the front door. We first saw Jim Zumwalt come in, then like an angel from heaven a mystical man in a white suit walked into the venue. We all straightened up and couldn't believe it. Zumwalt came into our dressing room first and said that he had Kalodner with him and he wanted to meet us. What you need to know is the night before Zumwalt told us, *"Listen, he might want to meet you before but probably not. Kalodner will only watch a few songs and leave. You won't have any answer tonight and don't expect much."* Before we could react, the man himself came in with a huge grin and his hand extended to shake. We were in total shock. After a quick introduction it was show time. We had the great idea for Jesse's 88 year old grandpa JP to do our intro. He is the same old guy who was sitting on the front porch with a shotgun in our Lumberjack music video. His job that night was to come out on stage with a pistol, say into the microphone '*Hey boys, there's some people out here to see you, want me to shoot em?"* Then he would fire six blanks into the air and we would kick in. We ran into a problem. We timed the intro at rehearsal, taking into account for his old age and how long it took him to walk from the side of the stage to the microphone. That evening, JP was sitting right next to us in the dressing room. It took him so long to get to the stage, we had to have our intro played twice before he even got to the microphone. I thought this was going to be a disaster but the show must go on. We hit the stage hard and by the second song Kalodner made his way in the crowd right between my mic and Jesse's mic. Standing right in front of me, John Kalodner was surrounded by drunken *Jackyl* fans in the middle of Georgia screaming their guts out. I was tripping at that point. I couldn't believe I had such a legend watching me play but we had practiced for it. He then pulled out the special notebook** and actively started taking notes while studying each of us individually. In that book, he was writing down our first singles, critiquing all of us, and putting the first *Jackyl* record on paper. (At this point, there was no way that Kalodner knew that the songs he had written down in his notebook were our only songs) Once the show was over, we headed back to the dressing room. Covered in sweat, we had a little laugh about the intro being all fucked up when someone came running in and said, *"They're coming!"* Then we heard a sharp knock on the door. Zumwalt came through first with the most excited look on his face. (In his mind, he's already spending his 20%) Kalodner was right behind Zumwalt with a big grin. Kalodner said in his classic John Kalodner accent, which is very distinct, *"You guys were great!"* He turned to Zumwalt and said, *"We're doing lunch tomorrow. Let's get lunch at the California Pizza Kitchen. The guy that owns it is a friend of mine. I'm going to sign these guys."* I turned to Jesse Dupree, *"Did he just say what I think he said? He said he was going to sign us?"* Jesse then turned to Kalodner and said, *"It's been a real honor to play for you. If I never see you again I just want to thank you for coming out."* Kalodner, still smiling, said, *"Are you calling me a fucking liar? I said I'm going to sign you. You just be at lunch tomorrow."*

We met the next day and signed a letter of intent because it was a Sunday afternoon and we couldn't sign any real papers until the next day. With that record deal, Kalodner had a few rules. We had to wait for Brenden O'Brian*** to produce the record and we had to wait six months until he was available. We had to stay on the road playing the same shitty gigs until we could record. We couldn't say a damn word to anyone until we recorded the record. That wasn't a problem until the dumb asses that had shitty little record deals were talking down to me for not getting signed. It really pissed me off but I persevered.

** *The Special Notebook – This is the legendary notebook that Kalodner used to outline in advance the making of some of the greatest albums in rock history.*

*** *Brenden O'Brian – All I'll say about him is this: Search Brenden O'Brian record producer on Wikipedia. It will amaze you. He also warned us about some managers and t-shirt venders that would screw us hard with bad contracts. He said to get wined and dined by them but don't sign a damn thing.*

I want to take this time to say something about John Kalodner. Kalodner would buy us anything we wanted to eat. If you wanted 20 lobsters, he would get you 20 lobsters. But he would only buy us one drink then we would have to buy them ourselves. He would not contribute to any kind of alcohol abuse or drug addiction. He had signed a lot of big bands that threw their lives away for drugs. I always admired him for that. The next time we saw John was when he flew us to LA for a week to really show us what the business was like. We wanted to make a name for ourselves at Geffen, and show Kalodner how much we respected him.

When we got our official tour of Geffen Records we all dressed up just like Kalodner and walked right into the record company. (As they say, beware of what you ask for). The biggest thing we learned about Kalodner is that he is brutally honest. If a song sucks, he'll say it sucks. If you're fat, he'll tell you you're fat. These were things we needed to know if we wanted to succeed.

The great John Kalodner has retired from the music industry and I have not talked to him in a few years. This is a personal note to you, John. *John I know you're not surprised that Jackyl is still around after 20 years because you told me we would be. You are the reason why. So thank you.*

Will the real John Kalodner please stand up!?

If electricity came from 'Arkansas', well that night it came from Memphis! The one and only, Jim 'Dandy' Mangrum of Black Oak Arkansas.

UP THE IRONS! On tour with Iron Maiden's Bruce Dickinson.

BAM! One of our Heroes, Evel Knievel!

Me and Queen guitarist, Brian May (one of my top 5!!). Intimidating night!

The 'Easy Rider himself, Peter Fonda and some guy they say runs a tequila and hair product company, the cooler than shit and inspiring, John Paul 'Mitchell' DeJoria.

Country boy, city boy! DAMN! Who would've thought it! On stage
with Rock n Roll Hall of Famer and RUN DMC's, Daryl McDaniels.

On tour with The Damn Yankees, on this day, Ted and I were seconds
away from doing a modern day version of William Tell! Yes, I was going to
let him shoot an apple off of my head!! Someone smart stopped us!!

CHAPTER SEVEN

LAWSUITS

I have three different stories about *Jackyl* being sued. Let me put it to you this way. We have a saying in *Jackyl*, *"If we didn't have to haul around all of the extra gear just to provide a great show or if we didn't have lawsuits against us, we would all be driving Lamborghinis right now."*

<> <> <>

The Longhorn Steakhouse Debacle

We begged and pleaded with Geffen Records to give us a budget of $15,000 to make our first music video for the song "I Stand Alone". We would film it in Atlanta because if we filmed in LA it would have cost over $100,000. Our 'Down on Me' music video cost $250,000 because all of it was filmed in Los Angeles. You have to understand that there are so many fees and extra needed bullshit in California it isn't even funny. We knew we needed to get creative with $15,000 to make our first music video kick ass. If you remember the orange van story, I alluded to one of our lawsuits. Buckle up because this is it!

The parental guidance sticker on our first record was a big controversy. So we took the opportunity to make our protest part of our 'I Stand Alone' music video. The first thing we did was pull in front of a K Mart shopping center with a tractor-trailer truck with all of our gear on the back of the flat bed. K Mart refused to sell our record because of the Parental Advisory sticker so they were our first target. Jesse was driving the truck around and I have no idea how he wasn't arrested because he had no trucker's license. The plan was to jump on the back of the truck, start playing music while filming it and have the police come shut us down. But after 5 minutes of playing, no cops showed up so we eventually called the cops on ourselves. The cops came and it was great publicity and really added to the video shoot. That was not enough for us though.

Our next genius idea was the day before we heard that a bunch of record company big wigs and local Atlanta 96 Rock DJ's were having lunch at a local Longhorn Steakhouse. This next target was conveniently only a mile down the road from the K Mart where we were shut down. We got the great idea of going into the restaurant, have Jesse crank up the chainsaw, run into the room where the record guys were eating, and saw their table in half. The film director told us the manager of the restaurant was cool with it. Our target was put in a private room to the side and everything was set to go.

We pulled up to that Longhorn Steakhouse in the orange van with film crew in tow. We kicked open the door and ran in. Jesse cranked up the chainsaw and we headed to the private room. Everything happened really fast and we didn't realize what we had done until an hour after the fact. There was only one problem; the regular patrons of the restaurant were not told a damn thing! There were everyday business men in there and all hell broke loose. I remember one guy in a suit jumping straight out of the window. People were diving over tables and the bartender jumped over the bar and hurt her knee. In the end, multiple people sued us and the bill came to around $1,000,000. So even before our first record was out and running we were in unbelievable debt.

Sitting here 20 years later I realize it wasn't a totally bad thing. If we made some shitty bland video that played on MTV those days, Geffen Records would have forgotten about us. But starting out like that, owing them so much money, they had to make sure our record made it. This was the beginning of one hell of an expensive education. The cherry on top that day was our video director. After filming, everyone (including the film crew) went to celebrate at The Cheetah strip club in Atlanta. Only one hour into the party we saw our video director being thrown out of the club. I ran over to the bouncers to see what happened. The formal charge was a serious one; masturbating in the men's bathroom. I guess all of the beautiful southern women led that LA man to the point of no return. How's that for your first music video?

<> <> <>

The Second Year of Rock College

Six or seven months after the mega lawsuit, our record was kicking ass. Geffen Records realized that we did not have a manager. I don't think Geffen would have noticed this because they didn't expect much out of us anyway. But when our second single 'Lumberjack' became super popular and our record was beginning to really sell, a manager was on his way whether we liked it or not. Our record was doing great in areas where a rock record would sell. But the thing that surprised us the most was that it was super-hot in places like Alaska, Oregon, Montana, and Washington State. The reason for this was there were a bunch of rural loggers loving the 'Lumberjack' single. I'm talking about tens of thousands of people buying our album just for 'Lumberjack'. That single was #1 on the Billboard Magazine Heat Seeker's chart for weeks. Success was on its way. We had managed to find a very well known manager that we thought we could trust. At the time we knew we didn't need him but we were forced into it by Geffen. Within 6 months of just shaking the new manger's hand we knew we had to get rid of this guy. Our personality and work ethics clashed severely. This drove Jesse Dupree out of his mind because Jesse was doing all of the managerial work anyway for free while this guy sat on his ass for 20%. Just to break contract we had to go through another $1,000,000 in legal fees and mystery tolls. To this day I don't really know where all of that money went. After that I learned two very important lessons. The first lesson was no outside managers. From that point on Jesse would be our manager and *Jackyl* was in control of their destiny. The second lesson was to have legal protection. We now have an insurance policy to cover any other lawsuits.

<> <> <>

The Legal Condom

Over the years there have been a few incidents that were close but luckily no lawsuits became of them. One show during the 'Lumberjack' song, Jesse cut the stool in half like he always does and smashed it. A security guard was leaning on the stage watching us. Let it be known that guard was not supposed to be there. All security guards were briefed and they were supposed to be watching the crowd. When Jesse smashed the stool, a piece of the seat went straight for the security guy's forehead. It hit him pretty good but he didn't sue. Another time, the promoter of a show brought his girlfriend up to a part of the stage where she wasn't supposed to be. When Jesse smashed the stool, he did it away from the crowd so no one out front would get hurt. Well this idiot was standing right in the danger zone where she should not have been and was hit square in the forehead. Notice a trend here? We weren't sued because it was the promoter's fault. The only time we had to use that insurance was during one Christmas show a few years back.

At the end of the show during the 'Lumberjack' song, the local radio station had provided us with a huge Christmas tree for the stage. The tree stand was two 2x4s put together in a cross. Jesse had cut the top of the tree off, which was just what the radio station wanted, and people were begging for pieces of the tree. What happened next was a complete accident. Roman Glick went to toss the little top piece into the crowd. What he didn't realize was that the top of the tree was attached to the bottom only by some Christmas lights. It was enough that when

Roman threw the damn thing into the crowd the bottom came with it. That 2x4 base swung around and hit a security guy right in the head. I have to say it fucked him up. Paramedics took him to the hospital and we just waited for the bad news. It turned out that he was a huge fan of the band and we apologized and asked him if there was anything we could do. He said he would be okay and after time, we all forgot about it. The statute of limitations was 3 years for that incident. About three weeks until that statute ran out we got a call from a lawyer who had seen a video of the security guy getting hit in the head and wanted the guy to sue us. To his defense the guy had been cool about the situation. Against his lawyer's wishes, he just wanted to settle out of court. All he wanted was money to pay for his medical bills that we wanted to pay for in the beginning. In the end we did settle out of court. After it was all over the guy sent a long apology letter saying that he was very sorry for the whole thing. We had no hard feelings over it and we're glad it's over. For our sanity and the fan's safety, we go above and beyond to make sure these things don't happen again.

CHAPTER EIGHT

MOST MEMORABLE GIGS

ZZ Top European Tour

As promised, we pick up here from Celebrity Sightings with the Billy Gibbons/ZZ Top story. I could not have known 14 years later, I would be reunited with my hero Billy Gibbons but under different circumstances. Back In 1995 we were on our first tour in Europe. After a few shows with Aerosmith we got the opportunity to open for ZZ Top in Switzerland. At that time we were in Germany and had to get back to Switzerland as fast as possible. We had two German bus drivers who would drive in 4 hour shifts all day long. The off driver would sleep in a hole that goes to the luggage bay on the bus. When one driver's break was up, he would crawl out of his cave and take the wheel.

After traveling all night, we got to the Swiss ski lodge where the gig was and oh my God it was amazing. Our rooms were incredible and they had given us each a gift bag containing all things Swiss Army. (Switzerland is the headquarters of Swiss Army knives) Everything was first class.

There must have been tens of thousands of people camping out for the show. People had been there for four days and one thing I noticed was there was not one cigarette butt or cup on the ground. These people picked up their trash and kept the area extremely clean. In America, it only takes one hour for an outdoor concert to become a disaster zone. We played at around 1 pm that afternoon with a bunch of European bands. I had never heard of them but the crowd really raised hell about them.

ZZ Top played around 9:30 that night. After we played we got to shake hands with Billy Gibbons and it was our first formal meeting. Even in Switzerland, ZZ Top had their famous Dancing Girls with them. While we were talking to Billy one of these girls came up to us and asked if we wanted to meet Dusty. (Dusty Hill, bassist for ZZ Top and the 2nd famous beard). I said, *"Sure"*. We went back to his dressing room with the dancer. We started chatting and the dancer left to "fix his plate". All of a sudden the dancer came back in with what looked like Thanksgiving dinner and two glasses of brown liquor. I said, *"Hey man if you're having dinner I can get out of here."* Dusty yelled back in my face, *"No! Stay! I'm just having a bite of dinner before the show."* He never took off his sun glasses as he engulfed the enormous amount of food and drained the two warm glasses of liquor. I shook his hand and said, *"Dusty, it was great to meet you."* He said, *"You too boy."* I left and let him prepare for the show. If you don't know, playing a big show is just like a hardcore work out. Can you imagine eating 6 cheeseburgers and running 5 miles? But he played flawlessly that night, and I was amazed.

After the show we ran into Billy again. We told him that our last show in Europe was in London two days later at the Marquee Club. He said, *"Boys I'll be in London on Saturday. I'll see you at the Marquee."* We showed up in London and checked into a swanky downtown London joint that the record company was 'paying' for. The next day we were going to play at the Marquise and the day after that we were headed back to America. I headed off to the gym that morning while the rest of the band hung around the hotel. When I got back to the hotel my brother was getting dressed up. I asked him what was up and he said that he was going out with Billy Gibbons. I said, *"Billy Gibbons who?"* Chris said, *"Billy Gibbons from ZZ Top dumb ass."* I said back, *"You're full of shit!"* After a few seconds the phone rang. Chris answered and said *"I'll be down in a minute."* He put a jacket on and headed to the door. Right before he left I said, *"Hey where are you really going?"* He answered, *"Out with Billy Gibbons. Look for yourself."* I got up from the bed and looked down into the lobby. Standing near the bar was Billy Gibbons. I saw him turn right towards me and shrugged his shoulders. I shrugged back violently and said to my brother, *"Holy shit, you weren't kidding!"* Chris said, *"If you're coming then hurry up!"* I took a shower and got ready as fast as possible. We headed down stairs and met Billy in the hotel bar. After everyone had a drink Billy ordered a cab for the 8 of us. He said it in a way only Billy Gibbons could. He went up to the concierge and said, *"I have 8 people in need of cabs this evening. I will have 2 cabs with pairs of 4. Two times four is eight. Eight divided by two is four. So, two cabs of 4, which is eight people."* It didn't stop there. He also said in the same strange tone, *"I also request some snacks for my skinny friends. I'll have some toast, four orders of it, with jam. We will also have some peanuts and some cashews too."* At that time, John Kalodner was pinching our sides and telling us that we needed to remain "cut" looking to get the money. Billy was the opposite. After a few brief moments, the concierge came up to him and said, *"Mr. Gibbons, your ride is here."* Billy whipped out his Davy Crockett moccasin bag and presented the Amex Black Card to the concierge. With a smile Billy responded with *"Excellent, we will be taking our snacks with us."* With two silver service trays the size of car tires, we got into our cabs and we were off. We did not know where we were going until Billy instructed our drivers to take us to the Hammersmith Odium. Billy instructed the taxi drivers to bring the trays back after they dropped us off. This was one of the most bizarre taxi rides I had ever had, it was insanely surreal.

We saw the country star/actor Dwight Yoakum play at the Hammersmith that night. He had his girlfriend Karen Duff with him, who was from MTV and starred in "Dumb and Dumber". Karen was very warm to a certain band member (I'm not mentioning any names) and when Dwight came out to see the two of them talking. Karen said, *"Hey honey! Are you ready to play?"* He said in an irritated tone, *"Uhh yeah! They paid me!"* Karen then ran back to the dressing room and was never seen again. At the end of that night Billy headed off with a group of guys and told us our rides were here and he would see us the next night when we played at the Marquee. We didn't hear from him all day and we let everyone know (security, etc) that Billy Gibbons would be coming to the show. We heard nothing from him and only after we played he showed up in our dressing room. He apologized profusely. We had to get out of there because we had a flight in a few hours. He told us that he would catch up with us back in the states. I thought, *"Wow what a cool ass weekend with Billy Gibbons."*

Once we get back home we were getting ready to go on a headlining tour. Within a day, Jesse got a call from Billy Gibbons inviting us to go on their '94/'95 Antenna Tour with them. Even though we had not played a single note in front of them, we had been hired to open for them. I learned later that Billy hired us because of one thing, our southern accents. On this tour, there were more of those dancers that I mentioned earlier. But ZZ Top's road manager gave us fair warning *'not to mess with the girls'*. He told us in a genuine tone that if we were to mess with one of these girls that we would be off of the tour. We were scared as hell and obeyed this rule. This was a power tour because we were selling out massive cities (New York, San Diego, Chicago, etc) and staying there for at least two days. This was the tour dreams are made of. But with all of the untouchables around, it was like being in a strip club for 8 months straight. It was cool but kind of terrible at the same time. We all loved ZZ Top so we did the best we could.

On the Antenna Tour we learned to love Billy for what he really was, an absolute eccentric. For example, on this tour he had a car carrier follow the bus just in case he saw a car anywhere at any time he wanted to buy. He actually made a man pull over who was in an old Cadillac and bought the car on the spot. And when we were playing in Sand Diego, we went to Tijuana for a shopping spree. Billy must have spent $5,000 in that Mexican town that day. Do you know how much shit you can buy for five grand in Tijuana?! Everyone in *Jackyl* got a personalized gift from Billy that day. It just goes to show not only is he eccentric but he is genuinely a great guy. I got a sword, a Mexican blanket, and five bottles of Mescal, each with a caterpillar worm floating around in the bottom of the bottle. If you don't know, Mescal is the Mexican moonshine. It tastes like tequila on steroids.

We managed to finish our first tour with ZZ Top and had an amazing time. I can't thank them enough. The Antenna Tour was the pivotal point in our musical career because we were exposed to so many influential people and started a big fan base as well. I saw this tour as furthering my college education. I saw talent, weirdness, passion, more weirdness, eccentricities (times 10) and good old sex, drugs and rock n' roll. We have played many shows with them since and we are still good friends. I look up to Billy Gibbons as much as ever.

<><><>

Woodstock '94 and the 10 Foot Penis

We had just returned from Europe playing with Aerosmith and ZZ Top to an average of 50,000 people a day when we were invited to play at Woodstock '94. Having our first record go platinum and our second was going gold, everything was becoming a blur. I'm not sure why we were invited but I think we were invited for a few reasons. The first reason was because someone from Aerosmith insisted. And the second reason I think was because John Kalodner had pulled some strings to have us play the largest gig in the world at the time.

We were driving in from Boston when we heard the lineup. Playing that day was *Jackyl*, Green Day, Nine Inch Nails, Metallica, and then Aerosmith. When we arrived at the gig there had to be a line of 50 buses in our way. So we did the sensible thing and passed them all. We pulled into a headlining spot because the Aerosmith guys said we were cool. The Metallica parking spot was already marked off by big scary guys in black jumpsuits. I learned to respect Metallica many times that day because they didn't fuck around when it came to their parking spot or their stage.

Our gear truck had already arrived and the crew was setting up. The stage was revolving so one band could play their set and then the stage would roll around for the other band to start. I was a little concerned because there was a large commotion around our equipment trailer. I ran up to see two dirty feet, wearing Birkenstocks, in the air with one of our road crew guys pumping his ass off. The guy had hooked up with one of the local girls and all of the Aerosmith crew guys were watching (around 40 dudes). This brought good will to everyone because some of the Aerosmith guys helped unload some of our gear in order to see this act of fornication. Once again *Jackyl* brought a large smile to a mundane day.

Other than musicians being backstage there were a bunch of venders showing anything from amps to guitars to tuners. On the way to the stage, Jesse eyed the Gibson vender and grabbed a brand new Gibson SG guitar. The guy behind the counter said, *"Hey! Where are you going with that?"* Jesse said slyly, *"Hey I play for Jackyl. I'm going to bring it right back. We play Gibsons and there are 350,000 people out there. I'm promoting your product!"* The vender just gave a weak OK and we were off.

As the stage rotated around I was extremely nervous. It's hard to describe the sight of that many people but it literally was as far as the eye could see. We got on stage and started to kick ass. In the middle of the set Jesse pulled his pants off and started to dance around the stage. On each side of the stage were huge monitors for the whole crowd to see the show. I looked over my shoulder to see Jesse's penis on the monitor. It was enlarged by 10 feet. People were gasping and it was hilarious! Sometime after that he sort of pulled up his pants and we did the "Lumberjack" song. He sawed a stool in half then set that bitch on fire. The crowed fucking loved it. Then for some reason, Jesse decided to jump into the crowd. We w looked for him but he had disappeared. Two road crew guys jumped in after him. One of these roadies that jumped in had an obsession of keeping his shoes white. He didn't really have enough money to get new ones nor the time to keep them clean so he spray painted them. The reason why I tell you this is when they finally found Jesse in the crowd and boosted him back on the stage, the last road crew guy had to be pulled back up onto the stage too. But when he got up, his shoes were missing! Somewhere in that crowd someone had stolen a pair of spray painted dirty shoes. Ha Ha! At the end of the show Jesse took our "shotgun" mic stand and shot. His other hand was holding the mic in front of the muzzle so when the blank went off the plastic wad shot out and shot the end of his thumb off. Blood went everywhere and the crowd was eating it up. Jesse screamed into the mic, *"Follow that killer!"* He then started to smash that 'borrowed' Gibson into a million pieces. At that point, all the other bands that were waiting to play or had played were lined up on the sides of the stage to witness our debacle. When *Jackyl* comes to play, just like Metallica we don't fuck around.

We headed back to the dressing room where paramedics were treating Jesse for his injured thumb. I should also mention that Jesse was hyperventilating too. We were told to turn on CNN, which was showing clips of us kicking ass and smashing that guitar. Jesse didn't lie to that Gibson rep; he really did get that publicity. We heard later that the big wigs at Gibson Guitars had commended the Gibson representative who 'gave' Jesse the guitar. *Jackyl* always brings the show in more than one way!

<><><>
100 Shows in 50 Days/21 Shows in 24 Hours

In our careers, we've had many publicity ideas (stunts) that
came to fruition. When Jesse was shot out of a cannon on the
"Full Throttle Saloon" TV show, we had been thinking of that
idea for 10 years. In 1998 we had the idea of breaking a world
record by playing 100 shows in 50 days. Our plan was to play two
shows a day. The first small show was in the morning and usually
in a Wal-Mart parking lot because we had a deal with them for
our new record. Local radio DJ's would spread the word about
what we were doing and they would hold a live remote broadcast
in each parking lot every morning. To constitute a show, the
Guinness Book of World Records stated that we had to play for
at least 20 minutes and we had to have a separate group of paying
fans each show. So we would pull into a parking lot, have all of
our gear set up on a flatbed tractor trailer, play our 20 minute set,
then send all of our gear to the big venue for that night. At the
start we had only 20 days booked. I got a little worried about this
but we thought once we got going the rest would come.

Near the end we were still 21 shows short. So this broke our
actual first world record; 21 shows in 24 hours. In order to do
that, we set up in a radio station in Abilene, Texas. They had a
little viewing room that held around 50 people. We would play
20 minutes, rest and talk on the radio for a bit then play again.
We started playing on the morning show and we ended on the
morning show the next day. I have to say the people who came in
the studio at 3:00 in the morning looked like they blew in from
crack town. But every show was sold out. So really, when we
finished in 50 days we played 104 shows. But our last show was
in Greenville, SC near my home town. There were fireworks and
25,000 people waiting for us at the final show but to be honest
the real 100th show was in some backwoods town in Mississippi.
So we started out trying for one record but we ended up with
two. We had no idea we had broken that second one when we
did. After the whole 50 day adventure we were $70,000 in the

hole and all we got were two pieces of paper. But I think the adventure was well worth it.

<><><>

WCW ... NWO

Once again I'm back on my fitness routine. This is where this story starts. From working out at a gym called Main Event Fitness in Atlanta, I've met most of the professional wrestlers of the '90's. Main Event was owned by Sting and Lex Lugar. We became buddies with Hulk Hogan, Buff Bagwell, Macho Man Randy Savage, Kevin Nash, Bill Goldberg, The Steiner Brothers, Sting, Lex Luger and Eric Bischoff. We hung out with all of these guys. With my side punk band Super V, we had just written a song called *New World Order*. Their wresting group was called NWO so it was perfect. Buff Bagwell told us that we should be their personal band in their pay-per-view special. So at the show the smoke rolled out and all of the wrestlers come out talking shit while we played. This was the first time I had played on live television with a producer telling us when to start and stop.

Hulk Hogan wanted to take my Les Paul and bash the "Big Show'" (another wrestler) over the head with it. I told him it wouldn't hurt the guitar but it would kill that large man. So what we did was take an acoustic guitar and cut the back out and fill it with baby powder. Hulk then came up to the band and grabbed that guitar from my stand and bashed the guy right there. It was great! It was the first time I had done a Pay-Per-View show with 10,000,000 viewers. The only problem with playing there was that the gear they got us was pure shit. The producer saw me looking critically at the gear and asked me what was wrong. I told him, *"Man I'm going to be honest with you, the gear is terrible."* There was no gripe from him. He didn't ask why or give me any bullshit. He responded, *"How can I fix it?"* In 30 seconds there were about 14 guys at our disposal with clipboards. They had written down everything we needed and went out to a music store to BUY everything we needed. This shows how much money these guys have! But the best thing I got out of this was that Hulk Hogan was a pretty good guitar player. Imagine that.

CHAPTER NINE

DEATH BY MISADVENTURE

A continuing joke in this book is the danger that the band/crewmembers of *Jackyl* are constantly in. Once again, just like pirates at sea, I am never sure if I am going to make it back to port. The drunken helicopter story was a cake walk compared to the danger in these next stories. *When Will I Die?*

When *Jackyl* was filming our fourth music video 'When Will It Rain' the first dangerous act happened. Because of our success we had a lot more creative influence and financial say-so to do what we wanted to do. There was a method to our madness. At one time on the tour bus we were watching a specific movie over and over again, "Cool Hand Luke". That movie stars one of *Jackyl's* favorite actors, Paul Newman. (Jesse Dupree likes "Hud" better.)

We filmed the first part of our music video in an old abandoned women's prison in downtown Atlanta. It was hot as hell in that prison and we were glad to get out of there. We moved to the country and did a mock scene from "Cool Hand Luke" where a fine looking woman starts washing a car in front of the prisoners who were in a chain gang working on the highway. The final scene of the video, the scene that almost got us, was taken straight from "Cool Hand Luke". In one certain part Luke escapes and dogs are hot on his trail. He had to swim across a river for the dogs to lose his scent. During the filming of "Cool Hand Luke" I'm sure they had stunt guys testing the waters before sending the actors across. Because of our *Jackyl* style of doing our own stunts, we just jumped right into the river. The irony here is so strong. The river we were swimming across had a huge current because it had rained a shit load earlier that day. When will it rain? Get it? More like when will I die?

When we jumped into the river, the current took us down stream immediately and violently. We all were literally swimming for our lives. I can see where people drown so easily in that kind of situation. The river had taken us downstream so far that we were way out of the camera's view. When we finally struggled out of the raging river we just looked at each other in silence. All of us almost drowned in that river that day. If we weren't southern boys who were used to doing stupid shit like that, there would have been five bodies washed up miles down the river. If we were to die that day at least our record would have sold 10's of millions of copies! But there would be no band that night to headline. Yes, after all of that, we still played our first sold out night at the famous Fox Theater in Atlanta, Georgia.

<> <> <>
The Sky Dome of Death
We were playing in Toronto opening for Aerosmith at the famous Sky Dome, home of the major league baseball team the Toronto Blue Jays. This place was so big that we pulled our buses and trucks directly into the stadium. When I mean this place was big, at 40,000 people it was considered half house. That morning I woke up inside of the Sky Dome in the back of the tour bus, looked out, and was amazed. This would be one gig that I would never forget, in more ways than one.

We were treated like royalty in the Sky Dome that day. I got to work out in the Blue Jays' personal gym. The show went off without a hitch and we kicked ass. Not only was the show amazing, we had our own posh hotel rooms to stay in that night. These hotel rooms were conveniently right across the street.

At our meet and greet, I met a couple of Canadian strippers that wanted to party. If you are not aware let me educate you. Canadian strippers (and prostitutes) are absolutely gorgeous. End of story, no problem! After the meet and greet with the fans we went over to the hotel to take a shower. Afterward, I was going to meet my two new Canadian friends at a bar down the street. This was a 5 star hotel and again I must emphasize that we were treated like royalty. Now let me set this up for you. This hotel was around 40-50 stories high. All of our rooms were on the 30th floor. We got into the elevator and this is where we had a kiss of death. This is where the evening went awry.

The elevator started to go up and of course we were jackassing around. We were pushing each other and jumping up and down. The straw that broke the camel's back was Jesse jumping on top of my brother Chris. Chris then tossed Jesse off of him. When Jesse hit the floor of the elevator there was a very loud screech/clunk and the elevator stopped immediately. We were stopped at the 22nd floor. I said out loud, *"Holy fuck!"* At that moment I thought I was going to die. There was no doubt in my mind I was going to freaking die. When the doors wouldn't open we pushed the emergency button and picked up the emergency phone. The people at the front desk told us they were going to fix it immediately. The phone rang 10 minutes later and they said the elevator had skipped its track and there was nothing they could do. The lady at the front desk told me on the phone in a calm Canadian accent, *"Sit tight, help is on the way. Whatever you do, don't move!"* About an hour went by and we were sweating bullets. The phone rang again. It was the head fire chief of the Toronto fire department. I'm talking about the head firefighter for the entire city. He said on the phone, *"Alright boys we're going to get you out. You're caught in between floors. We have to tie off the elevator then pry open the doors. You'll have probably about a 3 foot space to get out. Just stay put and do not move around."* So we stood absolutely still for about another hour. We could hear them above working in the elevator shaft. The phone rang a final time and the chief said, *"Get ready."* Then I saw these two metal clamps come through the doors. That's when I realized how serious the situation was. We were caught in between floors and it was pretty dangerous. Slowly, these "Jaws of Life" looking things started to pry open the doors. That's when we could see them. There had to be every single paramedic, firefighter and law enforcement officer in the city of Toronto packed in that hotel hallway.

They instructed us to lay down with our arms out and they pulled us all out of that little space, one by one. After we were saved the fire chief asked us, *"Boys, what happened up there?"* I shrugged and responded with an awkward smirk on my face, *"It just kind of stopped"*. All of these rescue guys wanted a picture with us because most of them watched us play with Aerosmith earlier. We were all visibly shaking during this photo shoot. I had all intentions of partying with the gorgeous Canadian strippers but I was so shaken up I went straight to bed. That night I had nightmares of plummeting to my death. I swear to God that morning when I went down to the bus, I walked down the stairs, all 30 stories. *Jackyl* cheats death once again.

<><><>

Billy Goat Gruff

This is not a story about physical death, but the death of the *idea* of *Jackyl*. This story happened a couple of days before the Toronto incident. We were in Vancouver, Canada and could have gone back into the US for a faster route to the next gig but the bus driver said we had to see this national park in the middle of Canada. That next morning after the Vancouver show I woke up to absolute beauty. On one side of the bus was a pristine forest as far as the eye could see. On the other side was an insane mountain range. This scenery was dotted with crystal clear streams and lakes. It was amazing. At that time of the morning the only people that were awake were me, the bus driver, and

Jesse Dupree. The rest of our sorry ass band mates were lying in their beds still drunk from the night before. To hell with them anyway, I never miss a chance to see the sights.

As we went down the road we started noticing a mountain goat here and there. Then we saw a huge heard of the goats alongside of the road. Jesse and I thought it would be funny to lure one of those goats into the bunk area of the bus and lock it in with all of our hungover friends. It was a perfect time to do it because we were the only people on the road. I asked the bus driver if it was cool to have a mountain goat on the bus. He responded, *"It's alright with me, but if that som-bitch shits or tears something up you have to clean it up!"*

Jesse grabbed a loaf of bread and we both stepped out of the bus. The bus driver was driving slowly next to us as we tried to coax the closest goat onto the bus. One of the goats started to get interested and began to get closer and closer. Cars started to come by and pass us. The strange thing was that the drivers of one of those cars were waving us off and pointing strangely. I had no idea what they were doing so we kept on coaxing the goat. Further down the road I saw the sign. This sign wasn't small, the word please was not used, and the sign was written in red. The sign basically read: DON'T FUCK WITH ANY OF THE WILD LIFE. NO FEEDING OR TOUCHING. SUBJECT TO A FINE OF $250,000 AND 15 YEARS IN PRISON.

As soon as I read the sign we got right back on the fucking bus. We pulled over a little further down the road. A hunter in a truck came up to us and said, *"They really aren't fucking around here. Watch out, there are a few park rangers coming down the road right now."* Imagine if we had kept messing around with this goat for another five minutes we would have been completely screwed. Half a million dollars and 30 years of jail between the two of us would have ended *Jackyl.* If we had been caught I would probably be getting out of jail right now, considering good behavior.

<><><>

While We're On Canada...

We were in Vancouver, Canada recording our second album 'When Push Comes to Shove' in singer Bryan Adams' studio. Our producer for that album was the late Bruce Fairbairn. He was well known for his work with Bon Jovi, KISS, AC/DC, and Aerosmith. We got into the studio and songs started to roll. We didn't even have to bring in our own weed because Vancouver has some of the most famous cannabis in the world. To set the stage, the studio is right next to Vancouver's insanely large port district. So we were in the studio recording for three or four days when one of the studio hands took interest in Jesse's shotgun microphone stand. For those who do not know, it is a regular microphone stand with a fully functional 12 gauge shotgun attached. Jesse shoots a blank at the end of each show to signal the finale. He asked me, *"Does he actually shoot this on stage?"* So I told him it was a part of our show and then this dumb ass asks, *"Can I shoot it?"* We go out to the back porch and Jesse Dupree's brother, Danny, loaded it with a blank. The studio hand held it in the air and shot it. It kicked like hell and everyone got a good laugh. Then we went back into the studio, smoked it up, and then continued recording. I was sitting at the producer's desk watching my brother Chris record the drum tracks. In a recording studio there are two lights above the producer's desk; a yellow one for a phone call and a red one for the door. This lets you know what's going on without interrupting recording. The red light went off, meaning someone was at the door. Mike Frasier, the engineer, asked me to go check who was there. It was late in the evening so I had no idea who would be there. I went to the door and slid open a little metal peep slot. Staring back right at me was the entire police force plus the fire department of Vancouver, Canada. I quickly slammed that metal slot shut and ran back to the producer Bruce Fairbairn. I told him the cops were there. He got up and actually opened the door saying,

"What is this?" As soon as he opened the door all of those cops burst in and told everyone to get against the wall. The police chief came in and said, *"Alright where's the gun?"* We all acted innocent saying we didn't have a gun and we didn't know what they were talking about. Then a police captain says, *"OK either you tell us where the gun is or I'm going to investigate that smell in the air."* (We had just smoked) Jesse then piped up and said, *"OK so I have a shotgun microphone stand."* The police had no idea what we were talking about so we showed him. They still couldn't wrap their minds around why in the hell we had it but they sat us down and explained why there were so many firefighters. The fire chief said, *"About 50 yards to the right of where you shot this thing off is a mountain of sulfur. If just one spark hit those chemicals over there, the explosion would have killed everyone in the port, including yourselves and probably burned down half of the city."* We then understood the magnitude of the situation. We told the cops how fucking stupid we were and sorry that it happened. We just escaped death and mass murder! In the end no one was arrested nor did they take the shotgun. I like Canada. I ended with a very apologetic, *"We won't do it again."*

<> <> <>

Unleaded

This is not necessarily a life or death story, but some funny shit. Plus it could have killed him!

Years ago the old bassist for *Jackyl,* Tom Bettini and I left a gig in Cincinnati in the old orange van. The rest of the guys were off with some girls or participating in some sort of debauchery. We were on our way back to the hotel. At that time, we kept the chainsaw and its gas mixture in the van with us at all times. That night the gallon jug containing the fuel mixture was sitting in between the driver seat and passenger seat. I was driving and Tom was chilling in the passenger seat. We didn't have a radio in that van so I put on my cassette headphones while I was driving.

Sometime down the road Tom gestures towards the jug and said something. I couldn't hear him because my head phones were wide open but I thought he asked if it was gas. I kind of just nodded my head and yelled back to him, *"Yeah!"* I saw Tom out the corner of my eye pick up the jug and take the lid off. I thought he was just going to sniff it or something but oh no! He turned it up and took two or three big chugs. I slammed on the brakes, ripped off my headphones, and yelled, *"Dude! That's gas!"* He looked at me in a way that only a man who had just drank gasoline would and said, *"I know! I thought you said it was sweet tea!"* We went straight to the hotel. He didn't want to go to the emergency room but he did the next best thing I guess. He called the hospital. The doctors told him to drink some milk, don't smoke for a while, and come to the hospital if he started to feel weird. Tom admitted to me later that his taste buds had been "fried" for years after that incident.

CHAPTER TEN

CHARITY WORK

Over the years, we have received a huge spectrum of food in our dressing room. When we first started we got a lot of loaf bread and a packaged meat. But now we get full turkey dinners in our dressing room . All along the way I've seen so much waste from a lot of bands. I have to admit, it takes a lot to make us comfortable on the road. The stuff we don't use we try to give to either opening bands or my favorite option; give it to bums. This brings us to the first story.

<> <> <>

My Man!

We were playing at the State Theater in downtown Detroit. I forget the exact date but this story happened in the middle of the winter. Because of the parking situation in downtown Detroit, the line for the show was stretching right in front of where our bus was parked. I was sitting at the front of the bus watching people go into the building when I saw him. It was a bum, a killer one at that. Now this is not a homeless person. Homeless people live in boxes and seem depressed. Bums walk with a certain kind of style. They go around and yell and wave at people they don't know, and then go investigate random things on the ground. As soon as this bum saw the tour bus and the line of people he had to check it out.

On the bus that day we had an overflow of Absolute vodka. I grabbed a bottle, a *Jackyl* t-shirt, and headed out. I had to put my hat down a bit because I had to walk in front of a few thousand fans. I was immediately recognized and everyone was trying to shake my hand when I got off the bus. But I was on a mission so I ran down the street to catch the bum. The first thing he asked me was, *"Do you got a dollar?"* I said, *"No but I have this."* I handed him the vodka and a *Jackyl* t-shirt. I told him, *"I'll give you $20 out of my pocket it you put this shirt on."* The bum was in shock. He looked at me, then the bottle of liquor, then at the t-shirt, then back at me. He then hit the liquor hard and said, *"HEEEEY!!!! Thanks man!"* I patted him on the shoulder and said, *"God bless you man"*. I ran back to the bus with fans high fiving me. The band then gathered in the front of the bus to watch him. He hit that liquor one more time and then put on the t-shirt. He went all the way down the line of our fans, thousands of people, and started singing our praises. He shook hands and tried to hug people, while still yelling at the tour bus how great we were. It was the best publicity I've ever seen.

<> <> <>

Christmas in July

Even in Connecticut it's hot as shit in the middle of summer. One day we were sitting on the bus when my brother Chris said, *"There's one of your boys."* I looked out to see a bum strutting down the street. He was classic, wearing brown checkered Sansabelt pants, a baseball cap, a belt that looked like it was from a woman's bathrobe and I swear the top from a mall Santa Clause outfit. I tried to get a care package for him but he walked off and we had to play very soon. I was a little sad that I couldn't help him. A few hours later after we played I saw him again, getting harassed by our security. He had changed the Santa jacket for a woman's bathrobe and I think into black pants too. I walked out and said, *"Hey let me talk to this guy."* I asked him, *"What's going on brother?"* He asked me in a rough voice, *"Do you have 10 cents?"* I figured that if he's asking for 10 cents then he's got $9.90 for some crack. I ran back onto the bus and asked my brother, *"Chris, do you have ten cents?"* Chris said to me, *"No but I've got*

$10". I went back to the guy with $10 and a bottle of bourbon. I handed him the liquor and money. He said, *"God bless you. You just saved my life tonight."* I said God bless you to him and slapped him on the shoulder. Dust flew everywhere. As soon as I said that, he booked it out of there. Probably straight to his crack dealer. Even the people in the parking lot yelled, *"Look at him go!"* I've never seen a man run that fast. Speaking of Santa...

<> <> <>

'Tis the Season

I have always loved Christmas. Every year I go out and buy decorations and personally decorate the bus. Usually, we take the entire crew out for dinner at Ruth's Chris or some expensive restaurant and we also have a Christmas party on the bus.

One night, about 10 years ago, I was feeling extra spirited. We were playing in Chicago and across the street was a porn shop. I had four special guys on my list (our road crew) and I checked it twice. I went in with an open mind but I had profiled each guy (in a good way). Roadie #1 loved porn books so I got him the most expensive fuck book in the store. But Roadie #1 is completely straight so it was only fitting that I got him a $50 homo erotic sex book. Roadie #2 has massively disgusting, sweaty, feet. He probably wears a size 18 or 19. The perfect thing for him was some weird flavored foot fetish spread that he would take home to his wife for her to lick off of his feet. Roadie #3 always boasted how he had tons of crazy, kinky sex with his wife so I got him a certain contraption. This contraption was a strap on dildo specifically for your forehead. Roadie #4 was a more difficult purchase. For this chronic masturbating roadie I got him an auto-masturbatory device. What it looked like was a hanging fly trap, the kind you pin to the ceiling and the sticky stuff rolled out. With this thing, you would roll it out, wrap it around your member, and then attach it to your waist. The premise was that it jerks you off when you walk around. My list was complete and I snuck each of their gifts into their bunks without a sound. It was a riot! That giving spirit evolved the next year.

Christmas came again; we were snowed in at a gig in Buffalo, New York. The only store within walking distance was a Dollar General. I entered the store with each roadie in mind.

This time, I got each of them something useful. Not that my last gifts weren't useful but everyone got Gold Bond anti-itch powder, candy, and socks. It's not Christmas without socks. Then I started to customize my gifts. One guy will eat anything so I got him a jar of 80 Vienna sausages, canned in Venezuela. Another roadie, who was dentally challenged, got a tube of tooth paste. One roadie who refuses to shower got ready wipes so he can wipe his damn ass. That year was more appropriate but not at my choosing though. If I could, I would make it a XXX Christmas every year but now it has become tradition that I go to the Dollar General and buy personalized gifts.

<><><>

The Souring of Humanity

This incident occurred during the winter in Cincinnati, Ohio. We had just finished playing at a gig. In the winter I'm usually more sympathetic to the homeless. I saw a fire in an alleyway near the club so I got a road crew guy help me bring a tray of food to these guys around the fire. I handed these guys a nice deli tray with different types of meats, cheese, and bread. Instead of thanking me, one of them just looks up at me and says, *"That's it?"* I just turned around and walked off. That made me realize that some of those people weren't just down on their luck, they were there because all they cared about were drugs and alcohol. That didn't stop me from giving though. It takes more than that to stop me.

CHAPTER ELEVEN

TALES OF A TRUCK STOP STORIES

If you look in the dictionary between Meth and Martians you will find truck stops.

<><><>

The Little Red Boots

Finding somewhere to take a proper dump is a real issue on the road. Even if you are in a million dollar tour bus you still can't crap in it. This fact puts you at the mercy of the next truck stop. This specific day I was woken up at 6:00 in the morning with the dire need to poop. Because of my rigorous workout schedule and a show every night, my metabolism was in overdrive. I ran up to the bus driver and told him to pull over. To my relief we pulled over at the next truck stop. There was fresh snow on the ground and hardly any trucks in the parking lot. In the bathroom I saw a row of 12 stalls that were freshly cleaned and empty. This is road-pooping heaven. I made my way to the very last stall and sat down on the last throne. I couldn't believe my luck. Just as I started my business I heard the door open. The sound of heavy footsteps and chains filled the bathroom. My joy turned instantly into horror, sprinkled with a mixture of fear and disappointment. This gigantic man walked all the way to my stall and tried to pry the locked door open. I said in a low tone, *"Someone's in here."* Quickly giving up, he moved right next to me. You must realize, he had 11 other stalls to choose from but chose the one right next to me. It happens every time and you know what I'm talking about.

As this huge man sits down the toilet creaks as he parks his mass. The sound of heavy breathing and my terror filled the bathroom. The man started to grunt violently and then opens the flood gates. The sound can only be described as that of a bloated cow being run over by a semi-truck. The smell was similar. I bent down slowly to get some recon on the monster next to me. To my immediate surprise I found him wearing an extremely small pair of red embroidered cowboy boots. When I say small, I mean these were probably a child's size 4. When I mean embroidered, these mother fuckers were fancy! I could see the girth of the man's legs overflowing the top of the boots so I knew this was a fully grown man with freakishly small feet. As I sat there with my pants down, I was in utter shock. This man must have gotten these boots specially made just for his terrible condition. Just as my mind began to wrap around the situation, "Tiny" wipes, flushes, and then marches his baby red cowboy boots out of the bathroom, never to be seen again. The worst part of it all is I never saw his face.

<> <> <>

Truck Stop Showers

Truck stop showers are one of the most decrepit places known to man. They are so disgusting you want to walk on napkins just to get in the entrance. On our Guinness Book of World Records Tour, we got to a point where we had to start using truck top showers. We pulled over at a truck stop right outside of Phoenix, AZ. That day the truck stop gods smiled upon us because this was the nicest truck stop shower complex I had ever been in. It was kind of like a nice hotel with brand new tile everywhere. Once inside, we all lined up in front of the shower we were assigned to. To paint this picture, generally in a truck stop the showers are lined up in a hallway with numbers above each shower stall. Each person is given a key to their subsequent shower. I inserted my key and everyone watched me as I struggle with my shower door. The knob would turn but the door would not open. Fed up with the bullshit, I shoved the door as hard as I could. The door gave way a little but slammed back shut. I opened the door quickly and looked in to see what the obstruction was. Here's your obstruction, a small naked Asian man, sleeping on the shower floor! I gave the door one more shove which sent the small Asian man across the floor. He hit his head on the toilet bowl with an audible *dink*. The naked Asian man jumped up and looked at me with a feral snarl. A black fella who worked there came running up to me and said, *"Sorry man."* The black guy then looked right at the naked Asian man and yelled, *"Look mother fucker, I told you to quit sleeping in these mother fucking showers!"*

CHAPTER TWELVE

GETTING EVEN

Like a hard headed idiot, I learned at a late age when someone insults you, you just can't beat their ass! If it is revenge you seek, you have to get back at a sneakier fashion. If you remember from earlier stories, when we got our first record deal we couldn't even talk about our deal for six months. At that time we had to deal with some real dick heads. Also we were still playing three 45 minute sets usually starting at midnight. In those days, the club where we played was Charlie McGruder's in Atlanta. It was the place to be. In this club we were the Lords of Rock. We were kicking ass and setting attendance records. Bands came to challenge us. It was a jungle. Blow jobs in the parking lot, fights in the bar and something I can confess now. To the manager Fred: (I think the statute of limitations is up now) The night the lights flickered and there was an "earthquake", that was us with a hand grenade. Sorry!

<><><>

Hairy Reed

It was a Sunday night and we were at McGruder's playing. Some guy who was a friend of a friend wanted to jam with us with his damn saxophone. We said okay. It was Sunday night so who gives a shit? The plan was we would let him come up at the end of the night, we would hold an A chord and he could jam a minute. When we showed up that night he was already back in our dressing room with his saxophone. He said he had tuned it, cleaned it, and he had stroked that son of a bitch with oil! He could have had sex with it for all we knew. But the bad part was, I had the feeling he wanted to play all night with us. Oh no, not going to happen. I told him he could play a few songs at the end of the night. He was upset but he accepted that. My friend Virgil, ex Air Borne Army Ranger (and generally insane dude) asked to hold the saxophone but the guy said, "*No! I already have the reed tuned perfectly.*" This dude was a total dork with a mullet. After he blurted that out he left the room. Virgil looked at me and our thoughts were one. Without a word we both dug into our pants and pulled out a clump of pubic hairs each. Virgil then said to me, "*Watch out for that mula-fucker.*" This meant that I was the lookout. We combined our pubes on the table. Virgil then removed the mouth piece from the saxophone and jammed all of our dick hairs into that reed and tightened it back up. It looked like a lady's fake eye lash was coming out of it. The dork came back just after we had put the saxophone in the case. Later that night we were playing and here he fucking comes. We held an A chord and watched the show. He started to blow and something was wrong. The sound was a little off but in between notes he started to spit out hairs. He kept doing that the entire song. It was hilarious! He was lucky though. If we hadn't put pubes in his reed Virgil said he would have broken his neck!

<> <> <>

Give Me Revenge or Give Me Death

Jackyl's old guitar player, Jimmy Stiff, was once insulted in McGruder's. It was over some petty bullshit, "*he said she said*" kind of thing. Jimmy was really pissed off and got Tom Bettini all riled up. At that point, Tom was ready to cut this son of a bitch. I told them to chill out. Jimmy wasn't the kind of guy to confront someone directly, but he was the master of sabotage. The guy who insulted him was the lead singer of the band that was playing that night. We weren't there to play, just partying. Jimmy got the idea to take a shit on their PA system. Tom said, "*Don't do that!*" so Jimmy got the better idea of taking a piss on their PA. When these assholes were playing Jimmy walked around to the back of the PA. He took a quick look around and whipped his member out and proceeded to drench not the speakers but the power amp rack. That powered the speakers and had a massive amount of electricity flowing through it. He had the happiest look on his face. It looked like he was watering his precious garden. Just then, my brother Chris came up and said, *"Dumb ass! If you make solid contact with the damn power source it could kill you!"* So we stopped him. I learned never to stop a man mid-stream because when I pulled him away he pissed all over my shoes. When we disappeared, the PA cut out and those dumb mula-fuckers' show was ruined. I bet to this day they are confused about what happened. So, if you ever played McGruder's in Atlanta around that time, well now you know.

<> <> <>

Our First Stain

At one of our last gigs at McGruder's Club before we took off to California, Jesse took the chainsaw and cut the *JACKYL* logo into the ceiling. It was fucking great. The last thing Jesse said into the microphone was, *"No mother fucker shall ever touch this! If they do, they'll get their ass kicked!"* That was our first stain that we left. We call a stain anywhere we play that ends with Jesse cutting into the ceiling or wall with the chainsaw.

A week goes by after that incident and we were doing pre-production in Atlanta for our first record. On nights off we would go back to McGruder's to party. One of those nights, Tom Bettini went to McGruder's with some girl to watch whatever band was there. Tom was laying low in the back of the club. This band must have planned it because they brought in spray paint and sprayed all over the *JACKYL* logo that was cut into the ceiling. Tom immediately called everyone in the band. They couldn't get a hold of me or Jimmy Stiff but everyone else went plus Jesse Dupree's dad, Rip. Tom snuck outside and waited until everyone showed up. When everyone was assembled, they kicked open the fire escape door that was located next to the stage. Our crew surrounded the stage and Jesse walked up to the singer, cranked the chainsaw and revved it right in his face. At this point the drummer started to cry. Jesse got on top of a chair and re-cut the *JACKYL* logo back into the ceiling. Jesse then grabbed the mic and screamed into the singer's face, *"DON'T FUCKING TOUCH IT!"* Til the day the club was torn down, no one ever dared touch that ceiling again.

<> <> <>

Who's Laughing Now?

A comedian friend of mine is sort of an asshole. He's not a bad guy but if a woman, strong drinks, or certain chemicals are involved then he might leave you stranded in the middle of nowhere. In fact, he did this to me so I owed him some assholery. I went to go see him perform one night with the thought of heckling him but that's not original and it happens to him all the time. This guy is a cheapskate. He won't buy himself a drink so he would ask someone in the crowd what they're drinking. Once he would get a response he would then say, *"Well I could really use one of those!"* Of course he did it and that was my in. I went up to the bar and ordered a shot of Bacardi 151 and asked the bartender to heat it in the microwave for 30 seconds and to pour it into a new glass. (So he wouldn't notice the heat). To give you some insight, Bacardi 151 is so strong it is literally flammable. The drink made its way on stage and my comedian friend asked into the mic, *"What is this?"* The bartender said it was from a fan. This cheap bastard didn't even think twice and he downed it. His face instantly went pale and he looked sick. The actual heat of the drink hit him first. I think he burned his tonsils. Then the burning of the high octane alcohol set in. He uttered out only one more sorry joke and ended his act. That's right ladies and gentlemen, I ended a comedian's act in 5 minutes with the power of one drink.

<> <> <>

Brush Fire

Many times on tour, my band mate and I (co-instigator) Roman Glick would get together to think up funny evil shit to do. If you do not know what a brush fire is I shall educate you. It is a shot of tequila with a few hits of Tabasco sauce. That wasn't hardcore enough for me and Roman. There is a hot sauce called Dave's Insanity. I shit you not, just a taste of it can ruin the next couple hours of your life. There were many times when people disrespected the power of the sauce. One time a guy said, *"This ain't shit!"* He then threw it all over his eggs and within 20 seconds he was on the ground with his throat closing up. He was literally moments away from a tracheotomy. Strange thing though, after they got a taste of the sauce they never showed their faces around us again.

Another time there was a guy 'disrespecting the sauce' and he said he could take a teaspoon of it. Once it hit his mouth he started to cry, like a little bitch. So we used Dave's Insanity to bump up the brush fire. So you know Dave's Insanity hot sauce is almost 1,000,000 scoville units. To bring it down to layman's terms, it's ridiculously fucking hot. It is 400 times hotter than Tabasco. We named this new drink the Hell Fire. If you want to get somebody back, get them a Hell Fire.

CHAPTER THIRTEEN

FROM FANS TO FRIENDS TO FAMILY

In this next section I am going to highlight some absurd actions our fans have done to meet us and the enormous lengths that we have gone to accommodate them.

We're So Sorry, Uncle God Damn... (Sing it to the tune of Paul McCartney's "Uncle Albert")

Back in 1995 we were playing a gig in Charlotte, North Carolina when a couple of fans came up to us after the show. They said they had a gift for us. It was a VHS tape with 'Uncle GD' written on it. Over the years fans and new bands have given us CD's, DVD's, and way back in the day plenty of cassette tapes. (Yes I'm that old.) As you can tell by now, nothing really shocks me. After the gig in Charlotte, I popped in that VHS tape on my tour bus. I can only describe this video as it was supposed to be funny but in reality it was tragic and cruel. This video was of a family in Shelby, North Carolina where a man, Uncle God Damn, was pranked/tortured by these two guys. I think they were his nephews. This was *Jackass* way before *Jackass*. They did all of these stunts without any payment, only personal pleasure. What would happen was that the nephews would pool together their money and buy gallons of liquor. Then they would feed that liquor to Uncle God Damn then fuck with him. By fuck with him I mean spray paint him, set him on fire and perform wrestling moves on the drunken old man. He would be so drunk that the only two words he could utter was *"GAWD DAYUM!"* (i.e. Uncle God Damn) In the videos it did not seem like he was hurt too bad but still he took a lot of abuse. I have to admit, at times it was funnier than hell. On our Guinness Book of World Records Tour, I got the privilege to meet this dear uncle. We were signing stuff at our meet and greet when he came stumbling through the line. His two nephews were basically carrying him. As a gift, we gave him an entire Big Gulp cup filled to the brim with vodka and presented it to the infamous uncle. I personally saw him drain the cup. Afterward he only slurred out, *"Gawwwwd Daaaaayum..."* Sadly, I learned that he died soon after our only encounter. If you do not believe what I am telling you then you can check them out at unclegoddamn.com or look him up on YouTube.

<> <> <>

He Wants Your Autograph

We were on tour with ZZ Top in New York City. We played at the Nassau Coliseum and had an awesome show. That night, Billy Gibbons wanted us to wait and leave with him. So later that night we left for the next show. We were pulling out of the venue when all of a sudden our bus driver slammed on the brakes, throws all of us to the floor and yells out, *"YOU STUPID MOTHER FUCKERS!"* I got up to witness a group of people who had pushed a quadriplegic/mentally challenged man wearing a *Jackyl* shirt in front of the damn bus! Let me specify, when I mean wearing the *Jackyl* shirt I mean it was barely stretched over his head. Our bus driver flipped out and yelled again at the people, *"Are y'all tryin' to get him killed?!"* I ran off the bus to see what was going on when one of the people pushing the man said to me, *"He wants your autograph."* They were literally going to throw their friend under the bus just to get our autographs. Even if that handicapped man had no idea who we were or where he was, he was having the time of his life. We were more than happy to oblige them and had many pictures taken. I always thought what they did was brilliant. It was a dumb plan but it worked. This will not be the worst fan stories ...

<><><>
Making a Case for MEDICAL MARIJUANA

A great source of information for this section of my book is our meet and greet line. I know it sounds redundant but yes, we do autographs for our fans after every single show. Now I've seen fans in wheelchairs, on crutches, and sporting plenty of casts. In this particular story, we had a guy in our autograph line, I swear to God, in a hospital bed! This man was in a full body cast and had his mouth wired shut. When his gurney was pushed up to our signing table, they wanted a picture with the band. Naturally I asked what happened to the guy. No shit, this guy was a lumberjack and a tree had fallen and crushed him. Sure, we do pictures for any fan. After this picture, the guy's wife said he had something to say to me. I said "OK" in a wary fashion. I leaned over and the guy just grunted. Like the classic cliché in a movie when someone is dying, his wife said I needed to be closer. I finally lean all the way over and put my ear right to his wired shut mouth. He grunted out, *"Want to burn one?"* This guy, who probably came right from the hospital to our show wanted to smoke a joint with me. I said, *"Hell yeah!"* The only problem and what I told them was that they had to get him and his rig all the way back to the dressing room. I felt for sure security was going to stop them or that his massive gurney just would not fit. I went back to the bus and changed my clothes. Lo and behold, when I returned to the dressing room he had made it! One of his friends lit up a joint and started to pass it around. When it got to the injured man his wife helped him slip the joint through his wire fence to take a puff. I could see the smoke seeping through his head cast! How's that for medical marijuana?

<><><>
A Nice Hot Bath of Salts

We were playing a bike rally and after the show, our meet and greet was pretty late at night, even for our standards. If you have ever watched The Full Throttle Saloon or have ever been to a bike rally then you know how weird the people can get, especially at this time of night.

A guy who was 300 pounds wearing only a speedo and devil horns is not that absurd to me. That night at our autograph line my brother leaned over to me and said, *"You're not going to believe this shit. There's a som-bitch that's coming here that's completely naked!"* If my brother ever says that, it means something was about to go down. I looked down the line and I didn't think he was completely naked until I saw his little pee-pee through the fence. When he got closer I asked some of the fans what was up with this naked dude. Some people told me they thought he was on bath salts. (The drug that makes you lose your mind) His eyes were wide and he was hyped. This was the first time in my career that I thought I was going to give a guy an autograph one second, and then have to beat his ass the next. I had no idea what was going to happen. As he got even closer I saw that he had 2nd possibly 3rd degree sunburns all over his body from being naked in the sun all day. It was a sight! So when he came up, I was in defensive mode. But when he started to talk, he was the nicest guy. It was like a politician trying to get votes. He would just say, *"Hey guys, great show! Thanks for the autograph! You guys have a great night!"* On top of that, he did this in a very orderly fashion, respecting us and the other fans around him. The one guy who's ass I thought I was going to beat was the best fan ... ONLY NAKED!

<> <> <>
Firewater

I truly mean it when I say I love Native Americans. My brother Chris and I are in fact part Cherokee Indian. Having said that, whoever said don't give alcohol to Indians was not fucking lying. Here's my in-field research to back up my statements.

<> <> <>
One Little...

If you have ever been on a tour bus then you know that the windows in the back lounge are very elevated from the ground. Because of that, you can yell something out of the window and no one can tell where the voice is coming from. It is like you can throw your voice. On this one occasion we were playing out west somewhere when Roman Glick and I noticed a huge, very muscular Native American man standing back stage. Next to the Indian I could see a rowdy group of drunken rednecks acting stupid and making everyone around them miserable. To this day I don't know why I did it but at that moment I yelled out of the window, *"Geronimooooooo!"* That huge Indian turned around and grabbed a redheaded redneck by the mullet and punched him the fuck out! He hit the ground, hard. Roman and I slumped down in the seat of the bus in a state of shock. I waited for about 10 minutes and popped back up. I expected cops and a huge melee but no, everyone was gone. That asshole redneck got what he deserved and in a strange way, I acted like the voice of God letting the Indian know it was OK to kick his ass. I still laugh when I think about it today.

<><><>

Two Little...

We were playing in Salt Lake City at a venue called the Salt Palace. This place was in the salt flats and it is awesome. We were hanging out near the bus before the show when we saw a massive Indian guy (6'8", 300 pounds) coming up to us for an autograph. We chatted with him a bit and he seemed like the nicest guy. He spoke in a quiet tone and he wanted us to sign his guitar. We had enough time before the show so I told him to go get his guitar from his car. When he got back we invited him on the bus (he had to duck his head down to get on the bus) and let him chill for a bit. After awhile he said he had to go back to the reservation. I asked why and he said, *"I have to go pick my buddies up and on our way back we are going to drink a gallon of liquor and watch the show."* I laughed off the comment as a joke then he left with his signed guitar. At the show that night, we were about three songs deep when it happened. From the stage, I saw near the back of the venue a huge melee had started. A few bouncers were being tossed about and security guards were rushing in. Then I saw him. The same huge Indian was being covered by bouncers trying to bring him down. Then the cops showed up. They got him all the way back to the double exit doors, which was his last stand. It was 20 degrees below zero outside, so the cold air from outside mixed with the hot air inside created a strange fog. I saw that he latched onto each side of the double doors with his huge arms and was not going to budge. Now the cops were there and were spraying mace in his face while beating him. Eventually there were too many and he lost his struggle. They pushed him into the snow outside and the doors slammed shut. This guy said he was a huge fan and went to every show in the area. After those doors slammed shut, I never saw him again.

<> <> <>

Three Little, Four little Indians

We were playing a gig somewhere in New Mexico and it was in the middle of the summer so it was hot as hell. During the show, two guys in the balcony were holding a sign saying, *"JACKYL ROCKS!"* Before the show the promoter said that there were a ton of Indians that were going to be there because we were close to a reservation. He also said, *"Get ready boys, they get wild!"* It just so happens that the guys in the balcony were Indians and were partying their asses off.

After the show we were winding down on the bus. Then one of our crew guys yells, *"They're stealing merchandise!"* Our bus driver runs out of the bus with his police sized Mag Lite flashlight in hand. He sees two Indian rockers in the bay of our bus with *Jackyl* t-shirts in their hands. The Indians immediately tried to run away so our bus driver whacks the first one in the middle of the forehead. He hits the ground and blood starts streaming from his head. The other one tried to get away so the bus driver hits him in the jaw. They both go down and the cops arrive. I then noticed it was the same two Indians holding the *Jackyl* sign during the show. The two Indians were cuffed and were questioned. By this time I had gotten back on the bus to watch out the window. All of a sudden the Indians were uncuffed. After they all talked it over I even saw our bus driver shake the hands of the Indians. When the bus driver got back on the bus he explained that they weren't stealing, they were trying to hide in the cargo bay to ride to the next gig. Our bus driver said that if the lack of oxygen didn't kill them, the carbon monoxide from the generators would have. So basically *Jackyl* has saved the lives of AT LEAST 2 Indians (by accident). So later that night we were pulling out of the gig with the bus going about 15 mph when we saw the same two Indians starting to run towards the bus. They both were still bleeding profusely from their faces and holding their sign. They were running next to the bus yelling, *"YOU GUYS FUCKING RULE!"* I couldn't believe it! I was laughing my ass off but the bus driver was pissed. He slammed on the brakes because they were crossing in front of the bus. The driver yelled, *"Hey you mother fucker! Get the hell out of here!"* The bus started to speed up and we left them behind. I can remember like it was just yesterday. I ran to the back of the bus to see the two Indian guys, still bleeding with their sign illuminated by the bus's taillights.

<> <> <>

May the Force Be With You

I am a firm believer in karma. You always reap what you sow. The next two stories will explain it a little better.

An Angel Gave Me $200,000

One day around 2002 or 2003 my phone rang. It was one of my dear friends. She is one of the smartest, richest people I have ever met. She has several college degrees and some of them are masters degrees. She can talk about topics that range from French art, to butt plugs. I swear to God. So she called me up and asked how I'm doing. The early 2000's weren't the best of times for *Jackyl.* Roman Glick had just joined the band but we were building ourselves up from scratch for two reasons. The first was the state of the music Industry at that time. The second reason was that two band mates had just left us hanging. So the phone call went like this: *"Hey Jeff, listen. I'm going to make this short and sweet. I've got $200,000 I want you to have."* I said, *"I can't take that!"* She responded with, *"You can do whatever you want with it. Make a new record or pay off your house or whatever. If you don't take it I'm going to go out into the street and give it to the first person that walks by."* I knew she was 100% serious about that because she had done it before. So I took that money and recorded the *Jackyl* "Relentless" album. This lady is also all about karma so I told her I would use this money to help more people than just myself. But I was not going to let my life's dream die. This was the boost we needed to keep us alive. We knew we had what it took to keep going, we just needed a lifeline. After our blessing from an angel, we made a deal with the...

Full Throttle Saloon

In *Jackyl,* everyone has their own specific interests and hobbies. By far though, Jesse Dupree and Roman Glick are the biggest fans of Harley Davidson and motorcycle culture. They are into riding their Harleys so much in fact that they follow the tour bus all over the country on their bikes. At one point they have ridden from Atlanta, Georgia to Sturgis, South Dakota and back. They only stop for gas and they keep that shit to the floor. During the mid-2000's the biker culture was at an all-time high with custom bike TV shows and televised biker build offs. Our first 10-15 bike rallies weren't too great for a few reasons. The promoters really did not know how to set up a big production. They didn't have the right stage, PA, light rig, or even a thought of a dressing room. I must say though that across the country, Jesse Dupree whipped some of these guys into shape. He would show them how to do a show properly and really help them out in the long run. So playing these rallies, it was inevitable that we would show up at the biggest rally there is ... Sturgis.

In Sturgis, there are two stages: The Buffalo Chip and The Full Throttle Saloon. The Buffalo Chip is the oldest and *Jackyl* actually played there first. After we kicked fucking ass there, one of our roadies came up to Jesse and said a guy was there who wanted to talk to him. That guy was Mike Ballard. Ever since Jesse met with Mike, we have only played The Full Throttle Saloon. The summer of 2015 was our 14th year playing there. Imagine playing the same night on the same date every year with every year getting bigger than the last. When we first started playing there it was very apparent that Mike Ballard had big goals. It was great because we needed someone like that on our team. Together we branded the biker scene while boosting each other up. Mike, Angie, and the entire Full Throttle crew are like family to *Jackyl* and there have been many nights where I knew we were more trouble than we are worth. I've had so many memorable moments at The Throttle. What happened next was only natural, The Full Throttle TV show.

A couple of years before it actually happened, Jesse told me, *"This place needs to have a TV show and I'm going to see it happen."* That he did. After the first couple of seasons it was obvious that the publicity from the TV show had put us on another level. Soon after The Full Throttle show, we got a call from Cartoon Network's Squidbillies*, asking if we would do a guest appearance. We said hell yeah! If you haven't seen it, go look it up on YouTube. (Squidbillies Episode: America Why I love Her) You'll get an education. Using the success of The Full

Throttle Saloon TV show we took Throttle on the road and Throttle Fest was born. To Mike Ballard, thank you. I have to apologize to Jesse right here. You were right about biker rallies and I thank you for it.

Some of you may know only a couple of weeks after our 2015 show, the Throttle burned down. We are all still in shock. If I had a magic wand I would have it back good as new in a second. But I have a feeling, especially with Mike's tenacity, that there will be a new Full Throttle Saloon and it will be bigger and better than ever!

CHAPTER FOURTEEN

THE ALIEN FILES

Going to Roswell

Ever since I was a little kid I have always been fascinated by UFO's, aliens, and Roswell, New Mexico. Of the many times we toured the American west I had never been to Roswell. You have no reason to go to that area unless it's specifically for Roswell. Roswell is well off the beaten path and it is difficult to get to. 150 miles out of the way just for a field trip normally doesn't fly with our crew. But one day in 2010, while leaving a gig in Lubbock, Texas, I was confronted by Jesse Dupree. He came right up to me and said, *"Happy birthday!"* I looked at him oddly and said, *"It's not my birthday."* With a grin he said, *"It is now."* He then informed me that we had the next day off and were going to visit that weird city of my dreams, Roswell, New Mexico.

While driving into Roswell I saw a sign on the side of the road that read *"Welcome to Roswell, Home of John Denver"*. Of all of the absurd shit Roswell could be known for, a guy who wrote the song 'Rocky Mountain High'? As fate would have it that my first time in Roswell was the 60th anniversary of the alien crash landing. There were thousands of people flocking to the city, some wearing aluminum foil hats just like the Mel Gibson movie 'Signs'. This entire festival was incredibly cheesy. It was like going to a really cheap beach without the ocean. All of the alien guys from the History Channel were there. It was a who's who for conspiracy theorists. After wading through this crappy festival, I made my way to a grilled corn vender. The lady running it was in her late 60's. She asked me, *"How do you like the festival?"* I told her I was little disappointed. She then said, *"Most of these venders are from out of town. They're just here for the festival."* I asked her, *"Are you from here?"* She said, *"Yep, I've been here all of my life."* With that I asked her, *"So what is your take on what happened?"* She paused for a second then said, *"My father was a fireman in the 40's and 50's. Never said he saw anything but he did say on that infamous night that something abnormal happened."*

<> <> <>

And the Mystery Continues

The story I'm about to tell you is 100% true. Some of the stories I've told in this book may have been stretched (just a tiny bit) but this is the truth. Through my life I have been very interested in the story of Roswell. On May 26th, 2014 we were playing at a bike rally in Houston, Texas. The show was great and we were signing autographs for fans. After about an hour or so my road manager came up to us and tells everyone we have to get going. The rest of the band went off to the bus and a guy who was in charge of a biker charity came up to me. He thanked us for supporting his charity and I told him no problem. The few minutes he held me up were enough for a woman to call my name. She yelled out, *"Hey Jeff! Can I please have a picture?"* I stopped and looked around. This woman didn't have a rocker look at all. She looked like a nurse who had just come from work. We took a picture and she said, *"Thank you so much, I've had one of the worst days of my life."* I asked her what happened. She said, *"I'm a caregiver and my baby died at 4 'o clock this afternoon."* I was a little shocked. She then said, *"Well, I say he was my baby, he was a 92 year old man who I have been carrying for the past 3 years."* I gave her a hug and my condolences. After a minute I said I had to leave. She called my name again. I turned back around and she said, *"Can I tell you something? You're going to think I'm crazy."* I said, *"Lay it on me, I've heard some of the craziest stuff out there."* She started with, *"Have you ever heard of Roswell, New Mexico?"* I said, *"Of course."* She continued, *"My baby was Jack Trowbridge and he was at Roswell when the aliens crashed. He made me promise when he died to tell the first person I see that it was all true."* I knew the story already but I wanted to see if she was bullshitting me or not. If she was a nut, the she was a very well educated nut. She told me the story. *"Jack Trowbridge and other Air Force officers were playing cards at Jesse Marcel's house when they got a call about some sort of unidentified crash.* (Jesse Marcel was the Air Force officer that gave a first-hand testimonial of the aliens/spacecraft.) She continued with her story. I am paraphrasing here and it went something like this...

"An emergency call came in and Air Force officer Jesse Marcel got up and told everyone to keep playing while he went to check it out. A few hours later Marcel came back and asked the guys to come outside and take a look at what he had in the back of his truck. There in the bed of the truck was the crashed spaceship with one dead alien and two live ones. All of the men, Trowbridge included, approached the truck and as they did, the aliens that were alive died on the spot. Jack Trowbridge said that there were only two real alien crashes in the world; the one is Roswell and another one that happened in Siberia, Russia. The Ronald Reagan administration had bought the wrecked spaceship from the Russians for billions of dollars in the 1980's. The aliens that crashed in Roswell were considered benevolent while the Russian crash was considered hostile. Any other UFO crash is a lie, used to muddle up the fact that there is life somewhere else other than Earth."

As she was talking, I heard someone say the bus was about to leave. I gave her one last hug and she handed me a piece of paper with the name Jack Trowbridge written on it. I got on the bus and I was about to call her crazy when I opened my laptop and looked up Jack Trowbridge. As the bus took off we looked the man up on the internet. I challenge you to go look up Mr. Trowbridge and listen to his story. I have no way of knowing if this is true or not but I know this woman believed *everything* she was telling me. With all of the insane stories I have told you about in this book, this is the one that I have the most trouble getting people to believe.

CHAPTER FIFTEEN

WALTER REED ARMY MEDICAL CENTER

I hope you have enjoyed the silliness in the book so far and had a good laugh or two. This collection of tid-bits, hilarity, oddities, and atrocities has been a cursed treasure that has taken me 20 plus years on the road with my band *Jackyl* to gather. But at this point, I have to tell you where my heart really is. This final story is going to take a more serious tone and is dedicated to those people who defend each and every American's freedom.

I come from a military family. On my mom's side it was all marines, fighting from Nicaragua to Korea. On my dad's side it was all army, fighting in the Battle of the Bulge, Korea, and Vietnam. During my life I have had the privilege of listening to amazingly historical war stories, stories about men who have taken lives and given great sacrifices for their country. During my life, I could not have had the freedom or opportunity to do any of the things in this book without our military protecting that freedom. I speak for myself as an entertainer; what we do (entertaining) is cute at best. Compared to what our American military goes through, we aren't shit. Around my neck I wear 14 Marine dog tags. I am asked about them all of the time. They were given to me by either the Marine themselves or their parents. I want to get this clear. I respect every single person that has served in any branch of the American Military but because of my family history I have a certain soft spot for the United States Marines. The Dog Tags are from Marines that have either been killed or severely wounded in battle. I guard them with my life and they are my honor to wear. The following story changed my life and my entire perspective of living in the freest and greatest country in the history of this earth. This freedom does not come cheap though, and here is why.

We were playing in Baltimore around 2010 when Jesse (Dupree) got a phone call from an old friend from his high school, a guy named Gary Love. Gary Love's son Todd, a Marine, was hospitalized at the time at Walter Reed General Hospital in Bethesda, Maryland. He had lost both of his legs and one of his arms while on patrol in Helmand Providence, Afghanistan. Gary had asked Jesse if we could come by and visit Todd because he was a big fan of *Jackyl*. We would do anything to help and support a wounded veteran. Because of the severity of his injuries I had to mentally prepare myself before I went in. This was not a regular hospital. First off it's a military hospital. Secondly, this hospital didn't have regular patients. This hospital was filled with people who were hurt on purpose by evil people. These people volunteered to defend us and were severely wounded in the process. When I say I had to mentally prepare, I mean I wasn't just going to casually see someone in the hospital. I was going to see a 19 year old kid whose life had been drastically altered to make sure I can play a gig next week and every one of you reading this book can go live your life and raise your family without fear.

As we approached the hospital, two Military Policemen (MP's) boarded the bus to check us out. We weren't being searched; they just wanted to check out a rock 'n roll tour bus. We were escorted by the MP's to the front of the hospital where we met Gary. I had never met him before. The thing that hit home at that point was I had my son Jesse (Worley), the exact age of Todd, with me to meet this wounded Marine. I could not imagine being in Gary's shoes. As a father, my heart was broken for the guy. It is impossible to imagine my own son being in that situation. So I met Gary (former Marine himself) and he led us directly to Todd's room. The whole time I was nervous because I didn't know how to react to a guy who just had three of his limbs blown off. Entering the room all of my anxiety left me when I saw him. As I walked into his room Todd was talking to some chick on the phone and moving himself around the room with his good arm and using pull-up bars. This was a guy who had almost everything taken away from him but he was still going at it. At that moment, Todd Love became one of my heroes. Gary said to Todd, *"Hey Jackyl's here."* Todd hung up the phone and put on a huge grin. We shook his hand and started talking. As soon as we conversed I knew he was cooler than shit. This young man still had his warrior spirit and no injury was going to stop him from living his life. Little did I know, this meeting was only the beginning of our friendship. Later that summer we flew him out to Sturgis, South Dakota to the Full Throttle Saloon to honor him on stage. We even presented him (with help from our good friend and radio DJ extraordinaire Johnny Dare) with his own customized three wheeled motorcycle that he can operate without any assistance from anybody because Marines don't need no fucking help! After that first meeting with Todd, I fell in love (no pun intended) with Todd and Gary Love. These are true men of honor. Todd and Gary you have no need to worry. I'm not going to say anything about the crazy shit that went on all of those nights at the Full Throttle Bar! Todd from the bottom of my heart, every time I get to hang with you, it is a fucking honor, Brother.

Walter Reed Military Hospital, Todd Love
(read the story). Top left is my son, Jesse
Worley. So glad he was with me that day.

THE AMERICAN DREAM

Friends, I have not been 100% truthful with you. This window into my life that you have read so far has not been the complete story. There was period of my life before I created *Jackyl* that was not only extremely important, it was a trial by fire that prepared me for my future lifestyle. The names of the very real characters in these Vignettes* have been changed to protect the innocent and appease the aggressors. Just so you know, I am Ricky and my brother Chris is Ray.

*Vignette

/vin'yet/

> A brief evocative description, account, or episode. OR Could or could not be the extremely detailed story of Jeff and Chris Worley's childhood friends and their off-the-wall antics. Sorry, Momma.

The American Dream

Sadly inspired by unbelievably true events!
Written by: Jeff Worley and Alex Massios

Overview

This is a story of two sixteen-year-old boys. One of them is of an upbringing that's entirely different from the other. Unknowingly separated for years by a small patch of woods and an extreme culture barrier, one boy would be changed forever. This story has action, adventure, compassion, sexual dysfunction, and learning how to get along with another species. It also shows the real south, for all of its beauty, backwardness, and even its genius. The characters are brutally real, and ignorant as hell. Some stories say they are based on true events, believe me when we say this shit is real, it's real! But beyond all of the outrageousness there will be real life lessons that everyone can relate to. This story will make you laugh, cry, look on with horror, go to church, and vomit in your mouth a little. Buckle up or unbuckle your pants for a ride that will change your life forever.

Setting

This story is set in the Deep South during the late 1970's. At the end of winding country road you will find the palatial home of the Morton family. Not one... but two 3/4 length, old ass mobile homes, aligned off kilter, stuck together with tar and roach bugs. Adjacent to that, an old rust covered tin building that is used to illegally repair cars. (Extra money under the table) This simple setting, its bizarre characters and environment is the birthplace of a story that seems from another world, because it is!

Character Bios

Jimmy Don Morton - The father, foul mouthed, usually unwashed (one bath a week), drinks coffee all day long and would use it as a projectile weapon against the kids. He collects disability from the government but to "screw the man" out of $20 a week he is an illegal car mechanic working out of his rusty garage. No matter his mood, Jimmy Don will respond to anyone with a sharp "BITE MY ASS!" or "GO TO HELL!"

Norma (Strawberry) Morton - Mother, short, pink complexion, fiery red hair, loud country voice, coke bottle glasses, and let the kids get away with murder. Her place of employment is The Sunny Brite Egg Company where she packs eggs all day every day. Her income consisted of half cash and half eggs. After the last Morton child spawned, Jimmy Don felt sexually deprived. As he put it, "NO ASS FOR Jimmy Don". Strawberry does not just think, she knows TV wrestling is 100% real and will defend it as such.

Jimmy Boy Morton – is the main character in this story. He's fat, smelly, and with the foulest mouth you have ever heard. Jimmy Boy has modeled himself after the professional wrestler THE AMERICAN DREAM "Dusty Rhodes". So much in fact, that he bleaches his hair white, gives himself a home perm, wears a cow-boy cut full length leather duster (jacket), and teaches himself to talk with a lisp like the famous wrestler. He constantly threatens bodily harm on everyone around him and is the "Billy the Kid" of the "Dirty Sanchez."*** In his mind, he has set the un-official record for the most viewings of Smokey the Bandit in human history. He is also known to be the Morton with the flatulence!

Earlene Morton - At 18 she is the oldest of the three sisters. She is mildly obese, white complexion, white hair, huge breasts, and sexually active to the point of pulling her healthy teeth for her wedding night in order to enhance fellatio. Earlene would show all of the boys in the neighborhood any body part for money, a dollar would get you far. She is a very violent girl, but will make your plate for dinner after slapping the shit out of you.

Misty Morton - At 17, she is the middle sister. While being the smartest and best looking of the Morton's but that's not saying a lot. Most of the boys in neighborhood would try to have sex with her but were lucky to get their fingers wet. She is the family cook, making all of their 7 rotating meals, Karo syrup and all. With one sister making her money by sexual favors, this sister would make extra money by doing other kids homework.

Kandy (aka Butter) Morton - At 16, she is the youngest of the Morton sisters, short, portly, with a Dutch boy haircut. She had contracted sleeping sickness and spent a year in coma after eating a banana containing Tsetse fly larva.** After awaking from the coma, she had to learn how to talk again which lead to a permanent speech impediment. Also sexually active and of a kind heart; she would give out blow jobs to the neighborhood boys free of charge as long as a thick coating of peanut butter was lathered on. This is how she got her nickname "Butter."

Ricky – He is the other main character and narrator. From a middle class family with a strict southern Baptist values, he had never met anyone like the Morton's before. Ricky met the "Dusty Rhodes" incarnate when Jimmy Boy saved the two brothers from a bully. After finding out they were separated only by a small distance, the two became friends. After meeting the family, Ricky just could not stay away. After the two completely differently worlds collided, Ricky realizes that he had crossed the extreme culture barrier. Though it is expressed very differently, family values are held high in both homes.

Ray - Ricky's younger brother, skinny, lanky, and at 12 he was the awkward bystander that unknowingly traded his childhood innocence for an education that could not be bought. Throughout the whole story, he never speaks.

** The Tsetse Fly lives by feeding on the blood of vertebrate animals and are the primary African biological vectors of trypanosomes, which cause human sleeping sickness and animal trypanosomiasis, also known as nagana.

***(Dirty Sanchez) The act of taking one's finger, digging in their sweaty ass, and applying the residue to the victim's upper lip.

Episode Synopsis
Episode 1
"Meet the Morton's"

After being rescue by Jimmy Boy from a bully (by using Professional Wrestler Dusty Rhodes' famous "Pile Driver" maneuver), Ricky and Ray are invited back to the Morton house to meet the family. As part of Jimmy Boy's reward, the Brothers agree to pay $1 to Jimmy Boy for their first booby viewing. After school the boys make a trail from their house to the Morton compound. Having never been there before, the sight of the mobile homes takes their breath away. The first person they meet is Jimmy Don. He explains to them that in order to eat they must do some sort of work. After washing rusty nuts and bolts in Kerosene for hours, Strawberry screams "JIMMY BOYYYYYY DINNERS READY." Inside, Ricky and Ray sit down for dinner with the rest of the family. They meet all of the 'lovely' sisters and have their first meal with the Morton's. (Hamburger Helper, Beef Stroganoff flavor) After a family discussion on the correct spelling of Elvis turns sour, a brawl ensues. After throwing a barrage of coffee at everyone (including the shocked brothers),

Jimmy Don shouts out through the battle field of hamburger helper "YOU'ALL GO TO HELL, GET THE HELL OUT!" After making his peace, Jimmy Don removes his dentures, and with his knife, removes cheesy hamburger helper from his dentures and sucks them clean. At this point in the dinner, Jimmy Boy, Rick and Ray exit the mobile home to which Jimmy Boy asks if they have that dollar for what they had talked about earlier. They give him the money and move to the end of the trailer. The two brothers stand on the tongue of the trailer and are rewarded with the sight of Earlene Morton's stretched out milk bags. As the boys are looking on, Jimmy Don opens the bedroom door and sees the boys to which yells, "I THOUGHT I TOLD YA'LL, GET THE HELL OUT!" The brothers retreat home, with thoughts of only sugarplums and Earlene Morton's titties.

Episode 2
"The Skeptic Tank"

Jimmy Don asks the boys if they are interested in making some extra money by digging a hole for the new septic tank. Unsure what will happen, they agree and Ricky and Ray spend their first night at the Morton house. Little did they know it included being lulled asleep by Jimmy Boy masturbating then being jarred awake at 3 in the morning by Jimmy Don murdering cockroaches in the kitchen with the heel of his shoe. Following a breakfast of canned biscuits, Karo syrup, and a stick of butter, work started on the project. The first instructions from Jimmy Don are "NO BODY USE THE SHITTER!" The boys grab rusty old shovels and begin working. About halfway through, the boys notice Earlene heading to the toilet. With Jimmy Don not noticing, the boys keep working with smirks on their faces. Out of nowhere the toilet flushes. Jimmy Don screams "GOD DAMMIT!!" and everyone freezes and stares at the exposed pipe with anticipation. With a few seconds in between: a little yellow water, toilet paper, and a bloody tampon hit the ground at their feet. With dread in their stomachs, Jimmy Boy screams out "Somethin' else is commin'!" At that point a 14 inch brown turd comes out of the open pipe, hangs in midair for a second, and falls to the ground at their feet. As if a grenade was thrown into a fox hole, the boys jump out with roars of laughter. Jimmy Don yells, "GO TO HELL YOU SONS-OF-BITCHES!" The boys are paid that night with the second Morton meal of Hot Dogs. After eating six hot dogs a piece, Earlene and Jimmy Boy get into a fight about the benefits of grapefruit juice and weight loss. Earlene tells Jimmy Boy he's a stupid son of a bitch, Jimmy Boy retorts with a Dirty Sanchez**. Jimmy Don tells everyone to "GET THE HELL OUT!"

Episode 3
"I CAN'T BELIEVE IT'S BUTTER!"

The boys (Ricky, Ray, and Jimmy Boy) meet at the Morton's house for a day of dirt biking. Jimmy Boy has been boasting all day about his 'bad ass' Kawasaki, yet when the brothers arrive he cannot make it crank. Being the genius that he is, Jimmy Boy diagnoses the problem as the gas line. As Ricky and Ray watch, Jimmy Boy grabs a random tube on the bike and begins sucking. Out of nowhere Jimmy Don emerges, kicks Jimmy Boy in the ass, and screams, "YOU STUPID SON-OF-A-BITCH THATS THE BATTERY OVER FLOW!" With a mouth full of battery acid, the boys run inside to Strawberry where Jimmy Boy is administered a stick of butter for his severely burned mouth. He begins to suck it in a fallacious manner while his sisters and mother watch. The suck show causes a brawl with Jimmy Don telling the boys to, "GET THE HELL OUT!" With Jimmy Boy's motorcycle not working, he jumps on the back of Ricky's and they ride off. With no more than half of a mile of Jimmy Boy dragging his feet, he falls off the back. Ricky drags his fat ass on the asphalt for about 50 yards. (That day Jimmy Boy was wearing his usual summer attire, Daisy Duke Shorts and a midriff cut shirt exposing his belly) The dragging incident had left Jimmy Boy without any skin from his ankles to the top of his thighs and from his belly button to his man-boobs. In extreme pain, Jimmy Boy cries and moans all the way home. At home Strawberry puts Jimmy Boy on the family couch and proceeds to rub his naked, scraped up, roadrashed body with butter. The boys eat their third meal with the Morton's. (Hamburgers) Soon a brawl breaks out with his sisters over Jimmy Boy lying exposed on the couch greased in butter. At which time Jimmy Don screams, "GET THE HELL OUT!"

Episode 4
"My Check"

On the last Saturday of every month the Morton's have their family outing which includes a trip to the flea market and dinner at a local grease pit. The only problem is Jimmy Don's disability check has not come. As time wears on, he is in mental agony. The longer he is away from his blessed check his alleged disability becomes magnified greatly. Without his check he isn't able to buy all of the junk he wants at the flea market. He becomes even more of a son-of-a-bitch by inviting the boys over for dinner and charging them for it. All most at his death bed, the check arrives and he no longer needs his cane to get around. The whole family including the brothers (Ricky and Ray) is loaded up into the Morton's 1970 Dodge Van equipped with their mandatory CB radio for a night out. (The Van was hand painted by Jimmy Don and Jimmy Boy with a paint brush)With Jimmy Boy at the wheel in his full Dusty Rhodes persona, he takes off like a scene from Smokey and the Bandit; driving half on the road/half off the road. Jimmy Don screams, "YOU SON OF A BITCH! GET THE HELL OUT!" Without stopping, Jimmy Boy gets out from behind the wheel and Jimmy Don takes over. As Jimmy Boy moves to the back of the van he administers two Dirty Sanchez's' to sisters Butter and Earlene leaving a slight brown smudge on their upper lips. The three smack each other in the face as the trip continues to the grease pit. Jimmy Don instructs everyone to stay inside while he goes in to order. He returns to the van with to-go boxes and they head off to the flea market. Inside the van its total peace and tranquility as they jam the burgers into their mouths. After an ugly scene of Jimmy Don arguing about a bid he lost, they leave the auction barn. On the return trip the Morton's horrible meat diet comes back with an evil vengeance. Jimmy Boy, with the most noxious flatulence and with his pants around his ankles, spreads his ass for a gas attack against his sisters. Just as they pull up to the Morton house chaos ensues. Jimmy Don slams the van into park and jumps out and screams, "GET THE HELL OUT YOU SONS OF BITCHES!" The brothers knew that was the signal to go home.

Episode 5
"Satellite"

Jimmy Boy gets his first car, a 1970 four door, six cylinder, Plymouth Satellite. Basically, it was a piece of shit! He boasted that it was 1970 Hemi Dodge Charger and threatened bodily harm if anyone touched it nor insulted it. After making a homemade hood scoop, adding traction bars and a CB radio, he painted it shit green with a paint brush. Jimmy Boy had the car of his dreams. It was half Smokey and the Bandit, half Dukes of Hazard. At this point, the brothers have invited Jimmy Boy into their world which includes playing on their church softball team. Unbelievably given the right pitch, Jimmy Boy could hit a home run every time (because he would practice ever night by hitting frogs with a baseball bat) and his Dusty Rhodes trash talk didn't hurt either. After hitting several home runs and winning the game, Jimmy Boy gets in his piece of shit Satellite and does a few victory donuts in the church softball field. The sight of Jimmy's shit green car spinning in the fresh cut field pissed off all of the church ladies. In the midst of the nice southern women Jimmy Don stands up and screams , "JIMMY BOY YOU STUPID SON-OF-A-BITCH!" At that moment the battery of Jimmy Boy's car is thrown into the engine fan causing even more sound and destruction. Jimmy Don, with cane in hand, hobbles out to the car and beings to literally kick Jimmy Boy in the ass. After towing the Satellite home using only the family Van and a garden hose as rope, Jimmy Don cleans house by instructing everyone to, "GET THE HELL OUT YOU SONS-OF-BITCHES!" Ricky then sends his younger brother Ray home as Jimmy Boy smuggles Ricky into Misty's bedroom for a dollar to spend the night.

Episode 6
"Please don't go over there!"

At this point it in the Morton Saga, has become apparent to the Ricky and Ray's parents that the boys have been learning horrible habits by spending so much time with the Morton's. (i.e., cursing, farting on each other, "Dirty Sanchezing", general wild behavior) The brothers want Jimmy Boy to spend the night at their house and the brothers' parents hesitantly agreed. As expected, Jimmy Boy causes a night of hell. First off he brings porno mags (which the brothers have never seen before) and are soon found by the brother's mother. Then Jimmy Boy clogs the toilet so bad he had to go outside and get a stick to un-lodge his mess. Then for a midnight snack, he eats an entire jar of mayonnaise with a spoon which adds to his chronic flatulence. At this point Ricky's dad said Jimmy Boy could never come back just because of his horrible gas. The next morning Jimmy Boy eats two sticks of butter for breakfast; this also makes the brother's mother angry because no one should eat that much butter. Soon a fight breaks out after Jimmy Boy gives out his infamous "Dirty Sanchez" to both of the brothers. In retaliation for this disgusting act, Ricky runs into the bathroom to find a half used Summer's Eve used disposable douche that his mother thrown in the trash. With an evil smile he attacks Jimmy Boy with it, squirting the contents into Jimmy Boy's mouth. The brother's dad runs them out of the house and screams, "GET THE HELL OUT!" The boys run into the yard almost to freedom when Ricky's mother calls him back to the front door and says, "Son, please don't go over there." But Ricky knows in order to become a man he must witness the WHOLE world including the Morton's.

To be continued...

ACKNOWLEDGMENTS

To anyone and everyone that I have come in contact with in
my life, thank you!
There are too many people to name and I'd wind up
forgetting someone anyway.
If you know me and I know you then thank you!
You made this book happen.
Edited by Julie Johnson
Edited by Trixie!
Editing and special thanks to Katie Bryan
Photos (front cover, back cover and page 5) by Kathryn
Reynolds
Permitted by Kathryn Reynolds
Photos (all remaining) by Jeff Worley
Permitted by Jeff Worley

Made in USA - Kendallville, IN
83768_9781533595195
05.13.2022 1334